ZR RIFLE

ZR RIFLE

The plot to kill Kennedy and Castro

by Claudia Furiati

Translated by Maxine Shaw

Second edition

OCEAN

Cover design by David Spratt

ISBN paper 1-875284-85-0

First printed February 1994
Second edition, 1994

Printed in Australia

Published by Ocean Press,
GPO Box 3279, Melbourne, Victoria 3001, Australia

Distributed in the USA by the Talman Company,
131 Spring Street, New York, NY 10012, USA

Distributed in Britain and Europe by Central Books,
99 Wallis Road, London E9 5LN, Britain
Distributed in Australia by Astam Books,
57-61 John Street, Leichhardt, NSW 2040, Australia
Distributed in Cuba and Latin America by Ocean Press,
Apartado 686, C.P. 11300, Havana, Cuba

Contents

Dedication

To Nei, Helena, Daniel and Fabián

And to so many others, too numerous to list, who have contributed to the creation of this work.

Thirty years after the death of JFK,
the Cuban State Security Department opens its files on
the assassination

"*The bringing to light of the truth about this atrocious murder is
the responsibility of the U.S. authorities. Our endeavors
concerning this case have been mainly directed at making it clear
to U.S. and world public opinion that we had nothing to do with
this horrible crime. We believe that the allegations of our
government's involvement in the assassination were aimed at
justifying a military invasion to overthrow the Cuban
revolution.*"

General Fabián Escalante

Author's note

This work is the fruit of an extensive study of information supplied by the Cuban State Security Department, together with books and newspaper articles, Congressional reports and "declassified" documents from the United States.

Structured for the most part as a narrative full of action and suspense, this text proposes to develop a theory on the assassination of President Kennedy. Our conclusions are drawn from the perspective of investigation and analysis, which obviously cannot cover all points of view, but does contain the essence of historical fact.

We hope that this book will contribute to the enlightenment of a deed which altered the destinies of both the United States and the world, and that it will lead to a profound reflection on the present day, where blockades continue to exist against free expression of thought and action.

Claudia Furiati

All excerpts quoted in this book have been retranslated into the original English from the Portuguese-language manuscript of ZR Rifle.

Introduction

Of all the fanciful literature produced during three decades with the aim of unravelling the conspiracy behind the shots that killed John Kennedy, it is most surprising that such contempt has been shown toward the investigations into the assassination carried out by Cuba. Possessing an intelligence and counterintelligence service whose efficiency is clearly shown by the physical survival of Fidel Castro — and no other political leader has survived so many attempted assassination plots hatched by the powerful CIA — Cuba was placed in the center of the scene of the crime by the very authorities charged to investigate it.

From the first moments that followed the 1963 assassination, the North American mass media have highlighted a great many versions, some using government sources, holding Havana responsible for the act which until this very day has been attributed to Lee Harvey Oswald. The Cold War, which in those days was at its height, helped to create the necessary atmosphere for the speculation, consecrated as if it were the absolute truth. All this benumbed public opinion in the United States and neutralized, under the label of a "discredited ideology," lines of investigation which pointed in other directions.

Time, more than any other factor, has pushed forward the evidence that Kennedy was the fatal victim of an alliance of forces and interests which opposed him. It was history that released Cuba from the prisoners' dock and that has made it into the principal witness into the Dallas crime — a witness that has still not been heard. What was lacking was someone to begin to provide Cuba with an audience for its evidence.

The great merit of the thorough-going study presented by this book is precisely that it reveals the hidden aspect of the Dallas assassination. By obtaining the first authorized access in 30 years to the Cuban Ministry of Interior secret archives into the Kennedy assassination, Claudia Furiati opened — as opposed to the efforts of hundreds of other investigators and journalists who have dedicated themselves to this topic — the reliable road to the truth.

During almost three months, the author lived in Cuba and totally dedicated herself to this investigation. It was a long time to be in exile, among the thousands of records, reports, photos, code names and maps — each day becoming more of a prisoner of what she discovered and of the striking images of the U.S. president being struck down in Dealey Plaza.

Before beginning her investigation, Claudia Furiati prepared herself in order to carry out her assignment with enthusiasm and efficiency. She devoured many of the books about the case and stored in her computer files hundreds of reports published in newspaper and magazine features about the mystery that she now sought to uncover. She became a specialist capable of sustaining whatever discussion about her inquiries and to rebut, using both logic and the facts, the inevitable rejoinders that her conclusions provoked.

Qualified in this way, Claudia Furiati could also critically analyze the great mass of unpublished documents that passed daily through her hands. From this material she extracted valuable information — many times revealing their sources — from the interviews with Cuban agents that operated in and followed, directly or indirectly, the anti-Castro groups in the United States. These anti-Castro groups were those responsible for carrying out Operation ZR Rifle.

One morning in October 1992, we were drinking coffee in the Hotel Capri, famous in another era because it was one of the favorite places of the Mafia when they frequented Havana during the dictatorship of Fulgencio Batista. Next to Nei Sroulevich, a supporter of the project from its beginning, I heard Claudia Furiati outline the first stages of preparing the book. It wasn't only an experienced investigator who spoke with great enthusiasm of the idea that had consumed her; nor simply the mature intellectual aware of her solidarity with the Cuban revolution. The captivation was that of a young student of 1963 who discovered, half unexpectedly, the challenge of having to write a work which would contribute to the clarification of an event which marked her generation and shook the world.

The manuscript of the book, ready more than a year later, demonstrated that the arduous search undertaken by the author had been enriched by her faith in the importance of her discovery. *ZR Rifle: The plot to kill Kennedy and Castro* will become a vibrant historical document, indispensable for those who wish to see, without filters of any sort, through the cruel lenses of the facts, the truth that for such a long time has remained hidden.

Nevertheless, a further six months were consumed in frustrating conversations in order to publish the book in the United States. Curiously, and here there is another surprise, the manuscript was always enthusiastically praised for the "originality of the work," "the seriousness of its preparation," and certainly its "sales potential." One by one, the initial doubts and prejudices around the work were overcome and the literary agents and U.S. publishers made plans and offers which, more than once, in a strange process of backing down, everything came to zero. It was a true blockade, only overcome after six months when Ocean Press of Australia made an offer to publish it.

Whatever provoked this incomprehensible and new blockade provides yet one more reason that makes *ZR Rifle : The plot to kill Kennedy and Castro* indispensable reading.

Ricardo Boechat

CHAPTER 1

Into the spider web of the unknown

Rain was falling in Rio de Janeiro and I stood perplexed in the doorway of the Roxy Cinema. I had just seen the movie "JFK" and I wondered why I, an ordinary Latin American, was so overwhelmed by those revelations; so many years of life and study have gone by, and yet it was as if I was encountering the story for the first time.

Sometimes life plays tricks on the generation of the 1970s, surprising us with some hidden reality. . . . Suddenly, a flash of memory brought me back to my childhood, to the emotion of that tense and solemn minute after the announcement of the assassination of President Kennedy. Now I understand that the child I was somehow sensed that this moment was a very significant one for the destiny of our America. It is the universe of that moment that I wish to relate to you.

Ever since then an **X** and a **Y** have been inside my head, making me dizzy and never leaving me be. In Oliver Stone's film, the mysterious character **X** provided a clue: the case of the death of JFK was related to General **Y** and to the center of dirty work at the Pentagon. Black deeds in the sense of the comment made by New

Orleans District Attorney Jim Garrison to his team: "White is black and black is white." The men in the white bull's-eye were the targets of the black operations. Then there was David Ferrie, the pilot who aided in the training of Cuban counterrevolutionaries, who insinuated in a rage one night that the people who killed **K** were the same ones who wanted to kill **FC**. An equation was being prepared like in the good old days of an algebra class. All that was missing was the **Z**.

Having been granted a multiple-entry visa, I decided to head for Havana, Cuba. I was possessed by an unhealthy obsession: What were these "black operations," whose name evokes such racism? Who were **X** and **Y**? What diabolical force would try to kill Kennedy and Fidel Castro at the same time? In Havana, among the mysteries, I would find some clues. In the beginning it wasn't easy. I looked up Alfredo Guevara, an old friend, part of the history of the revolution and a member of the Central Committee of the Communist Party of Cuba, and I told him my idea: I wanted Cuba's version of the Kennedy assassination. "Girl, what you want is almost impossible," he responded gravely. "But I'll see what I can do." I concluded that it was an affair of State. I wrote a two-page proposal to help persuade them and to keep my own spirits up. Days passed. There was more paperwork. And I waited. . . .

One afternoon I was summoned to Guevara's office. In the outer office I bumped into a tall, thin soldier who stood up courteously to greet me. I felt that somehow he already knew me, and before I could sit down in the only place available we were invited to go inside. We were introduced. I looked him in the eye and heard an imaginary voice whispering in my ear: "Your name is Bond, James Bond." On his ID badge two stars and an olive branch identified him as a Division General of the Ministry of the Interior. Then I stared at his dark glasses and a ring on his left hand that seemed to move all by itself. He asked me what I wanted to know. I explained my idea and my need to interview people and learn about the investigations of Cuban State Security into the assassination of Kennedy. Also, there were some other questions of a political nature. He asked me for time.

While I waited, I studied the documents already at my disposal. The readings I found most useful were the reports of the three official commissions that dealt with the Kennedy case: the Warren Commission, appointed following the assassination and named for its chairman (Earl Warren, Chief Justice of the Supreme Court); the Senate Committee, also known as the Church Commission (a 1975 investigation by the United States Senate into plans for the physical elimination of foreign political leaders); and the 1978 investigations by the U.S. House of Representatives Congressional Committee on the Kennedy assassination.

The Warren Commission began its investigations on December 9, 1963, after receiving five volumes of material prepared by the Federal Bureau of Investigation (FBI). It was created by President Lyndon Johnson, and included former Central Intelligence Agency (CIA) director Allen Dulles; Earl Warren; and Gerald Ford, a confidant of Richard Nixon, who later succeeded him as president of the United States. Fifty-one hearings were held over 10 months, thousands of documents were examined, and 552 statements were taken. The commission presented its conclusions on September 24, 1964: Oswald was the only perpetrator of the crime.

In spite of all the portentous apparatus put together for the investigation, the Warren Commission Report was nothing more than an affirmation of the previous FBI report, the U.S. Secret Service reports, and those of the Dallas police. Teams were set up to find out why Oswald killed Kennedy, but not if he had killed him; declarations and facts which deviated from this predetermined conclusion were discredited or glossed over; the evidence that supported it was emphasized and carefully prepared, even though it did not necessarily prove the conclusions. There were also declarations that never reached the commission because it was determined that they were not worthy of note or because they were never submitted by the police forces. Other information was retained by the CIA or the FBI to protect themselves. That was how the Warren Commission ended up doing an exquisite job of not clearing up the facts.

The Senate Commission, presided over by Senator Frank Church, was organized because of accusations that during the 1950s and 1960s the CIA carried out operations to eliminate a number of world leaders who inconvenienced U.S. policy. The Church Report confirmed that three heads of state had been singled out by the highest levels of the government as targets for assassination. These were Patrice Lumumba (prime minister of the Republic of the Congo), a young leader with leftist tendencies; the dictator Rafael Leonidas Trujillo, (president of the Dominican Republic), whose government considerably dirtied the hands of U.S. democracy; and Fidel Castro Ruz, the leader of the Cuban revolution.[1] Privileged documents were supplied by the intelligence agencies themselves — the CIA and the FBI — on which suspicion fell, and various closed door hearings were held with officials of these agencies; but the final report left unanswered the questions of who killed Lumumba and Trujillo and how the assassinations were carried out. The CIA insisted that their own efforts had failed and that they had no knowledge of or relation to these crimes. However, the Church Commission report confirmed that since 1959 the CIA had organized plans to kill Fidel Castro, their efforts culminating in a contract with the Mafia in the United States and three of its top gangsters: Sam Giancana (of Chicago), Santos Trafficante (of Florida) and John Roselli (of Las Vegas).

Curiously, some of the lines of questioning touched on the Kennedy case, and the members of the committee were subtly pressured to reinforce the arguments of the reprisal theory: that Kennedy's death had been Castro's revenge for the "humiliation" of Cuba during the 1962 Missile Crisis. At the same time, certain evidence pointed in the opposite direction, such as the connections between the activities of the CIA, Lee Harvey Oswald and anti-Castro Cubans, so that Senator Schweiker decided to form an independent committee to investigate the Kennedy assassination. Although some evidence was presented, such as the name of the senior CIA official called "Maurice Bishop," the Schweiker report (Investigation into the Assassination of President John F. Kennedy

---

[1] The Church Committee investigations also pointed to CIA participation in the assassinations of Mossadegh in Iran (in 1953), Ngo Dinh Diem in South Vietnam (in 1963) and the Chilean General René Schneider (in 1970).

— the Attitude of the Intelligence Agencies) arrived at few definite conclusions. The senator argued that no link between Oswald and the intelligence agencies could be proven given the denials of the officials and the lack of documentation in the issue; and the relationship between the anti-Castro factions and the CIA's plans to eliminate Fidel Castro was not explored,[2] even though these were among the points that sparked the investigation in the first place.

The house of cards built by the Warren Commission began to crumble under the weight of a growing number of investigations by U.S. researchers. In 1976, the House of Representatives approved the creation of a special House Committee on Assassinations with the aim of reopening the Kennedy case. Years later, on the morning of July 17, 1979, the chairman of the committee, Rep. Louis Stokes of Ohio, called a press conference to announce the completion of the final report — 686 pages and three volumes of appendices — which once more threatened to name various U.S. intelligence officials. Backed up by evidence produced by experts who reviewed images and sounds recorded during the assassination, the official conclusion contradicted — albeit timidly — that of the Warren Commission.

The report concluded that there probably had been a conspiracy to murder Kennedy, that more than one person (in addition to Oswald) had fired at Kennedy, and it acknowledged the connection between Oswald and David Ferrie. However, the committee failed in its efforts to uncover proof implicating the CIA, and it barely hinted at Mafia involvement. The report stated: "The committee believes, on the basis of available evidence, that the National Organized Crime Syndicate per se was not involved in the assassination of President Kennedy, but this evidence does not eliminate the possibility that individual members [of the Mafia] might be involved." Further on the report stated: "It is probable that neither Marcello [Carlos Marcello, a member of the Louisiana Mafia] nor Trafficante were involved in the assassination."

---

[2] The Warren Commission never followed this line because Allen Dulles, one of its members, was the director of the CIA when these plans were conceived.

Unknowns. I was drawn as if by a magnet to a strange world, full of intrigue. It was the first week of April 1992 when I heard the news that the FBI, under the pressure of public opinion provoked by the film "JFK," announced its willingness to reopen official proceedings on the assassination. Days later the U.S. Congress decided not to release the documents locked away with seven keys since 1978. Representative Stokes declared: "It doesn't matter what we release. We will never stop the speculation." Filmmaker Oliver Stone responded: "There can't be any evidence. Nothing is in writing." If this is so, I asked myself, what new or compromising information could be inside these famous 848 boxes and thousands of papers that Representative Louis Stokes has been sitting on for years and which will only finally be opened in the year 2029. The insistence on preserving the mystery only serves to reactivate suspicions.

In the middle of April I received a phone call from my Cuban James Bond, the general I had met in Guevara's office. He told me he wanted to talk about my project. We met. Since he didn't seem disposed to break the silence, I decided to comment on what I had been reading. I argued that there was a common backdrop to all the reports that linked Lee Harvey Oswald to the CIA, anti-Castro groups and the Mafia, that was the continual attempts against the Cuban government. The way I looked at it, I remarked, this was the road to follow. He listened to me attentively, and when I finished speaking, he simply told me that he agreed. I can't say whether or not my rosary of explanations was necessary to gain his confidence, or even if his positive response preceded his phone call. At any rate, nothing is gained by such speculation.

So, the interview sessions began. That first morning, considering my bad habit of always arriving 10 minutes late, I made an extra effort to be early. Even so, I discovered to my surprise that he was already on the premises. His inevitable sunglasses, carefully placed on the table, gave me the signal. Little details told me that he was allowing me into his world.

I was nervous. I was afraid of falling into the same trap as so many other researchers and others curious about the Kennedy case: that of disinformation. There were so many theories and false trails that I wondered if it was really worth trying to unravel the knots. Discreetly, he encouraged me to continue. After that it was impossible for me to stereotype him as the typical "spy." On the contrary, he showed me his human side: a personal magnetism, a firmness of principles, and a rare ability to tell a story. What stories? Memories of intelligence work. Tales of the G-2.[3] He became the Z, the key, and from then on he was no longer simply a James Bond.

Notes and computer printouts passed across the table. The room took on a strange, nebulous and stark air. Divisors of complex geometry filled the space, indifferent to the luxuriant garden that surrounded the house, and peeked through the windows as though to guard it. It was neither midnight nor noon. I had now begun my long journey through the narrations of the Cuban State Security Department, entering into the labyrinth of the Kennedy case, resolved to thread my way through the spider web of the unknown.

---

[3] G-2/DSE — Cuban State Security Department.

CHAPTER 2

From Pluto to Mongoose

The backdrop: Operation 40

The end of the 1950s. U.S. investment in Cuba amounted to a billion dollars, one eighth of the total invested by the United States in Latin America and Europe. It flowed from two principal directions: the massive capital of the powerful trusts and corporations such as United Fruit and Anaconda, that dominated the economy of the country; and the resources of the North American Mafia that sought to turn the island into the great tourist mecca of the Caribbean, a master plan springing from the famous secret meeting of Mafia leaders held in the Appalachian Mountains in 1954.

The Mafia, in a pact with the government of the dictator Fulgencio Batista, conceived the construction of a great chain of hotels and casinos, based primarily in the cities of Havana and Varadero, making use of all of the ports on the northern coast. Cuba was also being developed to function as a great aircraft carrier for the flow of drug traffic between Latin America and the United States. With the passage of time, the vacancy left by Cuba in this circuit would be taken up by the birth of the Medellin Cartel.

Around the middle of 1958, a series of episodes began to threaten that particular party and its very select group of guests.

The circle was closing in from all sides, and it was indiscriminate and inevitable. Many dissidents from all strata of society — the "high," "middle" and "low" — alienated for an eternity from power or displaced in 1952 by the dictator, had the Batista government in checkmate. Progressive victories of Fidel Castro's "barbudos" [bearded ones] in the Sierra Maestra and the underground movement in the principal cities made the men in power in the United States uneasy, especially those from the CIA. The inspector general of the Agency, Lyman Kirkpatrick, was sent to the island to contact their people in Cuba and reevaluate the direction of events.

On the basis of "privileged" information gathered by Kirkpatrick, fears began to give way to discord about what line of action to take. The officials operating in the "territory" (Cuba), more sensitive to the state of affairs and with an eye to the future, believed that the dictator would not be able to stop the advance of the revolution, and "common sense" told them it would be better to support other political forces which they might win over or those who were traditionally identified with the United States. But inside the central divisions of the CIA, Colonel King,[4] head of the Western Hemisphere department, advocated an unconditional alliance with the Batista government as the surest way to guarantee the protection of U.S. interests. In a pragmatic ploy, CIA director Allen Dulles outlined the following solution: maintain the existing alliance with the regime, but at the same time increase the penetration of agents in active opposition groups and in revolutionary ranks. His slogan, in a word, was infiltrate in order to reorganize the battlefield and try to influence the destiny of the movement.

Meanwhile, in January 1959, the revolution closed in and took power. The first measures taken by the new Cuban government to bring about the recovery of the national heritage — expropriation of land, public services and natural resources — and the executions (revolutionary justice) conflicted with U.S. interests. Those deposed

---

[4] Colonel King came from the Military Intelligence Service, and was linked to the FBI. He was a U.S. military attaché in Argentina, and was an official in the Eisenhower administration.

searched for a formula to retake control of the island. In a meeting held in May that year, Vice-President Richard Nixon, and the directors of Pepsi Cola International, Standard Oil, Ford Motor Co., the United Fruit Company and representatives of the Mafia made a deal: Nixon promised to overthrow the Cuban government in exchange for supporting his candidacy for president of the United States.[5] In Havana, James Noel, the new head of the CIA in the U.S. Embassy, led a team of 30 officials to recruit and train counterrevolutionaries. On December 11, 1959, an official memorandum from Colonel King to Allen Dulles proposed the elimination of Fidel Castro, the Cuban leader who "hypnotically attracts the masses," as a means to "discourage similar activities against U.S. possessions in other Latin American countries" and accelerate the fall of the regime.[6] In a meeting of the U.S. National Security Council (NSC) on January 13, 1960, Allen Dulles presented the "Cuban project" which, although it did not propose the "rapid elimination of Castro," did establish conditions for "careful planning of covert actions."[7]

Message decoded. The CIA began Operation 40, which took its name from the group formed under the auspices of the National Security Council — "the Group of 40"[8] — whose job it was to find a short-term solution for the Cuban question. Senior officials began the project and, after collective reflection, formulated the following plan: to provoke a "general uprising" of the Cuban people with the

---

[5] The article "The Kennedy Assassination — The Nixon-Bush Connection?" by Paul Kangas, a Californian private investigator, was published in *The Realist* magazine. This article attributes to Richard Nixon direct responsibility for the CIA invasion plans, in order to gain more financial contributions for his presidential campaign. Nixon promised the transnational corporations whose interests had been harmed after the triumph of the Cuban revolution — Pepsi Cola, Ford Motor Co., Standard Oil and others — and the Mafia, that he would help them remove Castro from power and that he would confirm the authorization for the invasion of Cuba as soon as he was elected.

[6] Report of the 1975 U.S. Senate Committee investigations into plans to physically eliminate foreign political leaders.

[7] Idem

[8] The group was sometimes called "Committee 5412," the number of the room in the White House where they met.

collaboration of the forces in exile and in this way "legitimize" a U.S. intervention. Later it was necessary to build a CIA base in Miami, where the majority of the exiles were based. Former U.S. President George Bush, at that time a "businessman," together with some of his business associates, mobilized millions of dollars in funds and resources for the operation, which was subject to no control whatsoever and did not go through any financial institution. It was strictly a cash operation.[9] For matters of an operational nature, Richard Bissell, the assistant director of "secret operations" of the CIA, chose his principal collaborators: Tracy Barnes was named to head up the Cuban Task Force to isolate Colonel King;[10] backed up by Frank Bender ("General Boulding"), a friend of the Dominican dictator Trujillo; Jack Engler, recalled quickly from Venezuela where he was directing the local CIA operations; Howard Hunt ("William" or "Eduardo"), author of espionage novels, himself the caricature of a spy and nicknamed "Uncle Sam" by the Cuban anti-Castro exiles because of the voluminous resources at his disposal at any time of day or night. It was Hunt's job to coordinate the Frente Revolucionario Democratico (FRD, Revolutionary Democratic Front), a coalition of Cuban exile groups that would serve as the political base for the invasion. David Atlee Phillips, named head of propaganda and communications for the Cuban operation, was a specialist in

---

[9] The article by Paul Kangas signalled that the Texan link of the CIA was based on the oil business. Through the machinations of Nixon, Texas millionaire George Bush provided support for setting up the operation, along with Jack Crichton, another Texas oil impresario. Two future members of the Bush administration also participated: Robert Mosbacher and James Baker. (Source: *Common Cause* magazine, March-April, 1990). According to a biography of Nixon, his personal and political relations with George Bush's family date back to 1946, when Nixon became an important part of his father Preston Bush's group, responsible for the creation of the Eisenhower-Nixon duo in the presidential election campaign of 1952. (Sources: *Freedom* magazine, 1986, L.F. Prouty and *George Bush*, F. Green, Hipocrene 1988).

[10] Richard Bissell, a university professor, an Ivy League graduate, and a sympathizer with the Democrats, feared the "hardline" methods of King. He tried to give the Cuban operation a structure independent from that of the Western Hemisphere department controlled by Colonel King, removing Allen Dulles from the CIA directorship and promoting Barnes to assistant director.

psychological warfare and the mass media, and had recently returned from covert operations in Havana, where since 1958 he had been recruiting agents. Traveling continually between the CIA headquarters in Langley, Virginia, and Miami, Phillips had to create the impression that the invasion was a spontaneous uprising of anti-Castro forces, manipulating the argument of a "betrayed revolution." An historic opportunity was launched for the CIA to begin its activities on an unprecedented scale: the preparations for the invasion would create a special relationship between its agents and the Cuban exiles which would later serve as the basis for operations on a larger scale, transcending presidents and historical time and space.

Bissell's team was composed of seasoned veterans of the Guatemalan operation of 1954. They planned to repeat the formula they employed to topple the democratic government of Jacobo Arbenz: to organize an expeditionary force outside the country and armed groups to serve as internal support for the invasion (the "fifth column"). On March 9, 1960, at a meeting of the Task Force, Colonel King's recommendations were presented: create the conditions to prove that Cuban leaders are preparing an attack on the U.S. Naval Base in Guantánamo (in the eastern part of Cuba) or "eliminate the leaders [Fidel Castro, Raúl Castro and Che Guevara] with a single blow"; otherwise, the present government "can only be brought down through the use of force."[11] Eight days later President Dwight Eisenhower signed a National Security Council directive on the anti-Cuban covert action program (Operation 40), whose premise was "the creation of a responsible and unified opposition to the regime of Fidel Castro outside of Cuba; the development of means of mass communication to reach the Cuban people as part of a strong propaganda offensive; the creation and development within Cuba of a secret intelligence and action organization which would be sensitive to the orders and instruction of the opposition in exile; and a large paramilitary force outside of Cuba for future guerrilla action . . . jointly with the

---

[11]   Report of the U.S. Senate Committee. Op. cit.

creation of mechanisms to provide the necessary support in terms of the logistics of the covert military actions on the island."[12]

The program was divided into stages: "Initially cadres or leaders would be recruited, after a careful selection process, and they would be trained as paramilitary instructors. . . . In the second phase, the cadres would be trained in secure locations outside the United States, with the objective of preparing them for an immediate attack on Cuba, and in this way to organize, train and lead the resistance forces recruited there, both before and after the establishment of one or more centers of active resistance."[13] The minutes of the meeting confirm that President Eisenhower promised to issue another security directive assuring that, from then on, none of the operations would have to be regulated. Some of the information on these planned covert activities has been in the files of the Cuban State Security Department for more than 30 years.[14]

At the Miami base the Revolutionary Democratic Front (FRD) was formed. Among the political figures heading up this exile coalition were: Manuel Antonio de Varona, one of the leaders of the Partido Auténtico (Authentic Party) which was in power in the two administrations preceding the 1952 coup by Batista (those of Ramón Grau San Martín and Carlos Prío); and Manuel Artime Buesa, founder and head of the organization called Movimiento de Recuperación Revolucionaria (Revolutionary Recovery Movement, MRR). Howard Hunt chose agent Bernard Barker as his principal assistant for coordinating the FRD and setting up houses for clandestine meetings. Barker was a U.S. citizen of Cuban origin who had served as a spy in Batista's police force and had been the link with Manuel Artime. Also on the Miami base was Frank Sturgis (Fiorini), a special agent. He had struck up a friendship with former Cuban President Carlos Prío, who was linked to the U.S.

---

[12] Report by General Maxwell Taylor: Commission on Studies about Cuba. USA. 1961

[13] Report by General Maxwell Taylor. Op. cit.

[14] *Actividades de la CIA contra Cuba antes y después de Girón* (CIA activities against Cuba before and after the Bay of Pigs). Report by General Fabián Escalante. Havana. January 1991.

citizens who ran the gambling casinos in Havana and who now lived in Miami and was eager to return to power. Through Prío, Sturgis had infiltrated Cuba at the end of August 1958 in the company of a Cuban pilot, Pedro Luís Díaz Lanz. His plane was destroyed and the following month he was able to slip back off the island with the help of the U.S. Vice-Consul in Santiago de Cuba, the CIA official Robert Wiecha. Preparing for a new trip in November 1958, Sturgis and Díaz Lanz were detained in Mexico.

A few days after the triumph of the 1959 revolution, Díaz Lanz was named the first head of the Cuban air force, and there is information which indicates that Sturgis attained the rank of captain in the same branch of the service. In September 1959 Sturgis fled Cuba and the following month he returned to bomb the city of Havana, alongside the deserter Díaz Lanz. In April 1960, Frank Sturgis began to direct the International Anti-Communist Brigades, a phantom organization that ran a network of safe houses, naval installations, a fleet of boats and planes, warehouses, the resettlement of exiles, and innumerable other activities, especially those related to paramilitary preparation in the training camps and support missions for anti-Castro exile groups in Cuba. Pedro Luís Díaz Lanz remained his faithful collaborator.

A month earlier, recruiting offices were opened for Cubans residing in the United States, seeking well-trained men. Later, all who applied were accepted. The pilots were chosen from within the Cuban community and among active duty professionals of the Air Force and the Alabama, Arkansas and Virginia National Guard. Cubans destined for clandestine work or espionage were sent to Camp Peary, better known in this secret world as "The Farm," a kind of CIA college where they practiced as frog men and received training at the "Isolation Tropic" base in North Carolina. For special assignments the best students were sent to the Trax Base in Guatemala, a U.S. preparation center for clandestine work; and then some went on to Fort Gulick, another nucleus of operations, located in Panama. Rafael García Rubio (a CIA agent infiltrated into the northern coast of Havana Province on March 23, 1961) explained when he was detained in Cuba: "Our job consisted of making contact with armed organizations and groups operating on the island, and training them in weapons and explosives. We were 86 men. . . . [O]ur last base was in Panama."

In August 1960, the operation's strategy underwent its first changes. Reports from agents in Cuba revealed a high level of popular acceptance of the revolution, and the CIA decided that it could not rely on the consolidation of the internal factor — the "popular uprising" — deciding instead to emphasize the external factor, the formation of the expeditionary brigade in Guatemala.[15] They gathered around $13 million to add to the fund for training and the arsenal of weapons, whose transport was aided by United Fruit and the García Line. By November, the brigade already had 600 men ready to embark for the Cuban coast as soon as the date was set. But new problems were emerging. "December 1, 1960, urgent. . . . [I]t is necessary to stop the political discussions and pacify the expeditionary force. . . . Nobody attending training sessions. . . . Awaiting instructions." Those were the words of the coded cable sent by the head of the Guatemala station to the central offices of the CIA.[16] In Bissell's office the officials looked worried. Time was passing. In addition, some of the counterrevolutionary groups that were to have acted as backup for the invasion — "the fifth column" — were being dismantled by the Cuban G-2 (later known as the State Security Department). It was not possible for a small brigade to carry out an invasion, even less one plagued with discord and indiscipline. The operation needed reinforcements, and the CIA decided to make a proposal to the Pentagon: prepare U.S. troops for "D Day."

Pause. At this moment code Operation 40 came up from the underground and into the light. It would no longer be a secret police force made up of mercenaries, exiles and other Cubans considered "suspicious" by the CIA in the United States, coordinated by the Cuban Joaquín Sanjenís.[17] It became an

---

[15] Report by General Taylor. Op. cit.

[16] Report from the Department of Investigations of the Cuban Revolutionary Armed Forces (FAR) on the activities of the Cuban counterrevolutionary groups in Guatemala. January 1961.

[17] Sanjenís formed part of the same group as Pedro Luís Díaz Lanz in the Cuban Air Force and was one of the first exiles to arrive in Miami.

"official" CIA operation at this point, incorporated into mainstream CIA activities. In the years that followed, Operation 40 was turned into a vast counterintelligence program aimed at "ideological cleansing." From propaganda to assassinations, it based itself on the counterrevolutionary groups and the Mafia, with its contraband and drug trafficking. Among the major players we find David Phillips, Howard Hunt, Frank Sturgis, Díaz Lanz, a handful of Cuban exiles and other North Americans, slowly weaving knots in the intricate spider web of covert operations that we are going to untangle thread by thread.

The same figures of this secret and underground organization would be the future "Nixon men," implicated in the Watergate scandal, and they would all reappear at different points in investigations into the Kennedy case. Operation 40 was transformed into an invisible but permanent backdrop on the stage of the drama of the CIA and U.S. groups defending the "establishment" from the example of Cuba within the rest of Latin America and other regions of the Third World.

The threads of Pluto
Signs of war. The Pentagon accepts the CIA proposal. As 1960 was coming to a close, the National Security Council approved Operation Pluto: land, naval and air military contingents totaling 2,000 men which would be ready to be called into action when the expeditionary force landed in Trinidad (on the southern coast of Cuba), and to take the region. Near this city lie the Escambray mountains, where it was estimated that armed groups controlled by the CIA could hold off Cuban troops and facilitate the movement of the leaders of a new provisional government, who would immediately ask for help from the United States. The attack was planned for a Sunday in the middle of April 1961. To complement the plan, the Eisenhower government would break off diplomatic relations with Cuba on January 3, "clearing the way" for the invasion. In the White House, the most enthusiastic supporter of the plan was Vice-President Richard Nixon, recently defeated by the Democrat John F. Kennedy in his bid for the presidency of the United States.

Kennedy was aware of the intentions of the CIA from July 1960, when Allen Dulles set up a meeting between him and the leaders of the Revolutionary Democratic Front (FRD). During the electoral campaign he found a good irrefutable issue, arguing that Eisenhower was passive on the Cuban question. Given the secret nature of the plans, he knew that Nixon would be prevented from giving any explanation on the planned invasion and his personal involvement. Appealing to the Cuban community in Florida, Kennedy urged "backing [for] the Cubans who are leading the resistance against Castro," "aiding the forces that struggle for freedom in exile and in the mountains of Cuba." Referring to the "red" base established 90 miles off the U.S. coast, he declared that communist domination in this hemisphere would never be negotiated. On November 18, 1960, immediately after his electoral victory, Allen Dulles and Richard Bissell rushed to Kennedy's summer house in Palm Beach to convince him of the importance of the plans already underway, although they did not fill him in on all the details.

In a meeting on January 28, 1961, six days after moving into the White House, John Kennedy and his National Security Adviser McGeorge Bundy received the first general instructions on the project from the Chiefs of Staff of the Armed Forces and the CIA. But the Kennedy team only became fully aware of Operation Pluto at the end of February, when they decided to alert the president. After analyzing the plans approved by Eisenhower's National Security Council, which included the participation of U.S. forces, Kennedy argued that they must be reevaluated by the Pentagon; that U.S. forces should not be used, since Trinidad was a very open area and everyone would know that the United States was directing the operation. The President was faced with an invasion planned for the near future, and even if he wanted to, it would be very difficult to cancel it since, in the year following an election, the political administrative structure of the country largely remains in the hands of the previous administration. Meanwhile, concerned with preserving the image of the country in world opinion, especially in Latin America, he made clear his opposition to the overt involvement of U.S. forces.

The Joint Chiefs of Staff of the Pentagon then proposed the Bay of Pigs on the Zapata Peninsula, instead of Trinidad, and maintaining a paramilitary brigade as the principal invasion force, with a U.S. military contingent as eventual backup. Kennedy approved the plan, now called Operation Zapata — but he reserved the right to veto it at the last moment.

In neither Miami nor Cuba was it easy for the CIA to establish the unity in the Cuban exile movement which was fundamental to the success of the venture. In Florida, the divisions were so great that it was necessary to find a political figure who could be respected by the leaders of the Revolutionary Democratic Front, and also attract other groups. They settled on José Miró Cardona, a university professor who had been prime minister at the beginning of the revolutionary government. By March 1961, other groups had already been incorporated, including the Movimiento Democrático Cristiano (MDC, Christian Democratic Movement), and the FRD joined the Consejo Revolucionario Cubano (CRC, Cuban Revolutionary Council). Manuel Artime was chosen by Howard Hunt and David Phillips as the political director of the invasion.

Then they were left with solving the problems of the Cubans "on the inside." Various CIA agents were already working inside the island to regroup the forces, but power struggles and the expectations of high positions in the future government impeded an accord. In the second half of February 1961 a meeting was held in Miami with several leaders who had recently left Cuba, and the same divisions arose. The alternative found was to assign the posts, and people linked to Antonio Varona and Manuel Artime were named to fill the main functions of coordination in Cuba. But this failed to resolve the disputes that remained when they returned to the country.

Artime's MRR, which operated in Santiago de Cuba and Guantánamo Province, were part of a plan to attack the U.S. Naval base there. One hundred and sixty mercenaries, being trained in New Orleans, Louisiana, under the command of Higinio Díaz[18]

---

[18] Higinio "Nino" Díaz was a Cuban officer who deserted from the Rebel Army.

were to disembark in the area of Baracoa in Cuba's Oriente region, pretending to be revolutionary troops, and advance on the base together with the on-island organizers of the attack. This was the plan that the CIA and the Pentagon had "up their sleeves," hidden from Kennedy, to create a pretext for the intervention of U.S. military forces as the main brigade arrived at the Zapata Peninsula.

Meanwhile, between March and April, as the time for the invasion approached, the principal counterrevolutionary leaders were arrested in Cuba and the groups in the Escambray mountains were disbanded. The following days were tense and frantic: the CIA not only lost their major means of communication, but also their control over the internal networks, which increased the disorganization and shattered the parallel plans. This information could not be passed on to Kennedy, and emergency meetings were held among CIA officials in Florida and in Langley, Virginia, in search of a solution. In a final attempt, the Agency decided to send a group of agents to try to rescue the detained leaders.

Capsules — Case No. 1[19]

While the preparations were being made for the invasion, the most secret aspect of Pluto was to take place: that of the famous capsules. It all began back in 1960 when the CIA decided to eliminate Fidel Castro. Richard Bissell took the initiative of contracting organized crime to handle the case, but since he didn't want to involve or inform his subordinates, he decided that the job should be directed by officials from the Security Office (which investigates suspicious officials and was under his administrative jurisdiction), although he himself would remain directly in charge of it. Colonel Sheffield Edwards, head of that department, was called in and he gave the job to the official Jim O'Connell.

O'Connell had an acquaintance named Robert Maheu, an old CIA collaborator on small missions, and a member of the FBI in his youth who later opened up a private detective agency in New

---

[19] An account created from excerpts of the report of the U.S. Senate Committee, op. cit., and materials from the archives of the Cuban State Security Department.

York. Jim O'Connell met with Maheu and told him: "You have relations with the Mafia. . . . [T]he Mafia has to take charge of this. . . . Who would you recommend for the job of killing Fidel Castro?" Maheu responded, "I know John Roselli." "Then we'll give him the job," replied O'Connell.

Robert Maheu, duly authorized, went to meet with John Roselli, linked to Sam Giancana, head of the Chicago Mafia, and to Santos Trafficante of the Florida Mafia. In the decade of the 1950s, the three had participated in the "discovery of Cuba" as a base and a route for the flourishing drug trade, as an abortion center and other activities which were considered illegal in the United States. His links with labor unions and figures from the Cuban government before and during the Batista administration date back to this time. Roselli, an expert in these matters, questioned Maheu, "Hey, who's behind this?" Maheu responded, "A U.S. economic group that suffered losses in Cuba." "Well, if this isn't an official matter, I'm not going to offer my services," Roselli challenged. "This is a very delicate matter. . . . I want to meet with someone who can guarantee that it's an official matter. OK?"

Maheu returned to Jim O'Connell who consulted with Colonel Edwards. Edwards authorized O'Connell to meet with Roselli. O'Connell then met with Roselli, using the pseudonym of "Jim Old," an Englishman who claimed to represent a "U.S. group." After O'Connell left, Roselli commented to Maheu, "That man is from the CIA. Level with me. I know that this is an official question, the government. . ." Maheu nodded affirmatively, giving the green light to begin.

Several meetings were then held in New York and Miami between O'Connell and Roselli, Trafficante and Giancana. The Mafia was offered a contract for $50,000, practically a symbolic figure, considering that their investments confiscated in Cuba amounted to tens of millions of dollars. The first idea, an urban cowboy gangster-style attempt, came from Sam Giancana: ambush Fidel Castro on a street corner in Havana and machine-gun him down. The CIA accepted the suggestion and they tried to recruit someone in Cuba who could "deliver the message;" but by the time they were ready to assign someone to carry out the mision, they realized that it would not be easy to arrange a shooting of the kind they were accustomed to, due to Fidel Castro's security system.

In December 1960, at a meeting with Jim O'Connell, Roselli argued that the CIA had to come up with a clever way to give the assassin at least a minimum time to escape. O'Connell took the problem to Colonel Edwards, who passed it on to Colonel King and Bissell, who requested the head of their laboratories, Joseph Schreider, prepare a suitable poison with the desired properties: one that would kill, but with a sufficiently delayed action to give the person who administered it time to escape. Schreider had already produced some poison capsules back in September, when Castro went to New York. By January 1961, Schreider had new capsules ready in the form of little nylon bags which contained a "synthetic botulism," a very active substance that dissolved only in cold liquids, left no apparent traces, and only began to have an effect two or three hours after ingestion. The problem was that handling the capsules was dangerous: if the assassin touched them or didn't wash his hands well, he could be contaminated.

Finally, in February 1961, the capsules were given to Roselli, who then went to Florida to meet with Santos Trafficante. The latter went looking for his old collaborator Tony Varona (Manuel Antonio de Varona Loredo), a well-known figure from the Cuban Authentic Party, whom, as we already mentioned, was one of the leaders of the FRD. He was the last president of the Cuban Senate during the administration of President Carlos Prío Socarrás (1948-1952).

In that era, through the positions he held, Varona established the best of relations with the Mafia, helping them acquire property and guaranteeing them police protection. He was also a business associate of the "capos" Meyer Lansky and Santos Trafficante in the ANSAN, a corporation which acquired land in southern Florida at low prices through extortion. When Batista took power in the coup d'etat of March 1952, all of the members of the Authentic Party from the deposed government fled to Florida, where they spoke out against Batista and supplied arms and money to some of the opposition groups. Some revolutionary leaders made contact with the "Authentic" leaders of the era; the former trying to obtain resources, and the latter trying to manipulate the revolutionary movement in order to destabilize the Batista government and return to power. With the triumph of the revolution, Carlos Prío, Tony Varona and other "Authentic" figures returned to Cuba, accompanied by José Alemán Gutiérrez. They stayed there for barely six months, after which time they decided that the plans of the new government were incompatible with their own.

The month before the Bay of Pigs invasion, Varona was already the vice-president of the Cuban Revolutionary Council. The selection of Varona as the man to take the capsules to Cuba in March 1961, was not only due to his good relations with the Mafia, but also because he had a counterrevolutionary organization in Cuba called "Rescate" (Rescue) which would take responsibility for the internal organization of the capsule mission.

The most ironic thing is that the CIA, which turned the job over to the Mafia in order not to be linked to the assassination of Fidel Castro, didn't realize that the Mafia would select someone from their own cadres in Florida. Moreover, when he accepted the deal proposed by Trafficante, Varona suspected that it came through one of the CIA channels, but because he had disagreements with Howard Hunt, the official in charge of organizing the FRD, he did not talk to him about the matter. On March 11, 1961, in the luxurious Boom-Boom Room of the Fontainebleau in Miami, taking advantage of a televised transmission of a boxing match featuring Joe Patterson, the following persons held a meeting: John Roselli, Robert Maheu (the CIA intermediary), Santos Trafficante, Sam Giancana and Tony Varona. According to Maheu's testimony before the U.S. Senate Intelligence Committee in 1975, he himself opened a suitcase, took out $10,000 and gave the money to Varona together with a cloth containing the capsules, which he pulled out of his pocket. Varona then tucked away the package and the money. The job was then formally proposed with an important addendum: the sponsors — read, CIA — insisted that the action not be carried out until they gave the signal. After agreeing upon the deal, they watched the heavyweight championship fight, had a few drinks, and enjoyed themselves.

In reality the $10,000 represented nothing more than a token payment on the part of the CIA since the Mafia had already contracted Varona for one million dollars. The entire business had clearly marked interests and was a completely illegal, underground operation: an obvious farce, from the use of pseudonyms from beginning to end, to the amount of money they were playing with in the game. The CIA person who always dealt with Varona was Maheu, but neither of them ever revealed their true identity to the other. Also, due to the compartmentalization of the Agency none of the men who met in the Boom-Boom Room knew that Varona was a CIA man and involved in the plans for the invasion.

At the end of March 1961, Varona called the Havana home of one of the leaders of "Rescate," Alberto Cruz Caso, and asked him to send a front man of absolute confidence to Miami. At that time there were regular flights between Havana and Miami every 45 minutes, so the courier arrived quickly. Varona gave him the capsules and a long letter for Cruz Caso, outlining complete instructions. The items were delivered the same day and "Rescate" began to look for the right place and the right person to carry out the attempt, and to make arrangements in two of the group's cells: employees of casinos belonging to Santos Trafficante and the "Peking" Chinese restaurant. It was well known that Fidel Castro occasionally patronized both the "Peking" and the Havana Libre Hotel (the former Hilton), attending important guests and delegations from other countries.

Remember that the plan could not be executed without the CIA signal, as agreed in the Boom-Boom Room. "Rescate" continued making arrangements in Havana and Miami. In the days preceding the invasion, the CIA official who attended the so-called Cuban Revolutionary Council in Miami, taking his directions from the heads of the Agency, received orders to gather everyone slated for the future government of Cuba — including Tony Varona — and isolate them in order to avoid leaks and to have them on hand. On the nights of April 13 and 14 they were confined to the barracks of an old Marine base south of the city called Opa-locka. Tony Varona was perplexed. Meanwhile, Robert Maheu, who was in charge of giving the signal, but who knew nothing of the actions of the CIA official at the center of operations in Miami, called John Roselli on April 14, and told him, "The order for the execution has been given." Roselli rushed out to find Varona, but couldn't find him anywhere. The Agency, with its strategy of "uncoordination," had not told the officials of the Cuban project the names of the persons in charge of the most delicate part of Operation Pluto.

Others factors contributed to the collapse of the plan: Fidel Castro, who knew about the invasion, was at that moment totally involved with organizing the resistance, and wasn't going out at all. "Rescate" was left without communications and without knowing which direction to take: the hotel, the restaurant, or some other place. Around the middle of April, the Cuban G-2 increased its arrests of the Havana-based counterrevolutionaries who were preparing to aid the invaders. Several members of "Rescate" were detained, and some capsules apparently ended up in the toilet. The capsules were destined for tragic comedy.

Kennedy and the Pluto disaster

All of this was the backdrop for the invasion expedition, which on April 17 landed on the beaches of Playa Girón on the Bay of Pigs. The 1,400 men who landed were defeated in 72 hours by Cuban resistance.

Weeks earlier, Kennedy received a telegram from Colonel Jack Hawkings, the military coordinator of the brigade, who was in Puerto Cabezas, Nicaragua, the spot selected as the launching site for the invasion. Hawkings informed him that everything had been arranged according to presidential instructions; but this was not the truth. Kennedy was ignorant of key aspects of the operation: the brigade was meant as little more than a portable detonator, insufficient by itself. The internal support for the invasion on the island had been knocked out, and air attacks by U.S. forces were indispensable. He was also kept in the dark about the biggest secret of Operation Zapata, in place since Pluto: that the CIA operatives were to dispatch the brigade at any cost, since the military chiefs at the Pentagon had guaranteed military action after the invasion. They deduced that, faced with the pressure of the moment,

Kennedy would end up authorizing military support in order to avoid humiliation.

According to President Fidel Castro, approximately a million Cubans were mobilized, counting both regular forces and the militia. When the mobilized Cubans were already destroying the expeditionary contingent, General Charles Cabell, deputy director of the CIA, called President Kennedy and asked permission to provide air cover for the invasion. Aircraft carriers with fighter planes on the runways with their motors running were positioned near the Zapata Peninsula, but the President would not authorize U.S. military action.[20] The means of deployment and provocation hidden up the sleeve of the CIA also failed: the group of 160 men trained in New Orleans and under the command of "Nino" Díaz didn't have the nerve to land in Baracoa and march to the Guantánamo Naval Base. They arrived to guard the coast, but when they were informed that government troops were on a nearby highway, they decided to flee.

Almost two years later, when the prisoners of the invasion were freed by the Cuban government, the major proof surfaced that the CIA was operating on its own and against the instructions of Kennedy. José Pérez San Román, head of the "mercenary" expedition, and other survivors of the invasion testified that CIA advisers from the Trax Base in Guatemala had promised them military support. Also, Colonel Frank, a CIA official, had revealed to Cuban commanders of the brigade that "forces in the administrative branch of the government were trying to cancel the invasion," but that if this were to happen they should seize the U.S. advisers, continue preparations for the attack, and he would give them instructions on the final plan and when and how they should proceed to Nicaragua. Ignoring certain conditions of the program and disobeying presidential orders, the CIA had caused a major defeat for Kennedy who found himself obliged to tell the world that he took full responsibility for the actions. He was furious with the Agency — not for planning the invasion, but for going beyond their limits. He accused the Agency of having gone forward with a

---

[20] Hunt, E. Howard. *Give us this day*. New York. Arlington House.

plan created and approved by the Eisenhower administration and of having put him "up against the wall" without giving him the proper information. He was also furious with Fidel Castro who, upon exposing the failed invasion, had publicly embarrassed him. Castro later reflected, "The Girón [Bay of Pigs] plans presupposed the use of military forces against Cuba. . . . The mercenaries sought to create in our country a kind of Taiwan, installing a provisional government. The United States military forces were already three miles from the coast, ready for action. . . . Kennedy, concerned about Latin America, and aware of the military and political error, decided not to give the order for intervention."[21]

A conflict arose: many high officials of the Agency held Kennedy responsible for the defeat. They insisted that there would not have been as many deaths and that the 1,200 men would not have been captured if Kennedy had not refused to use the armed forces. The CIA tried to cover up its responsibility. Agents quickly flew from Washington to Miami to conceal from family and friends of the members of the expeditionary force the real number of dead and to urge silence on the issue, alleging reasons of national security and the future liberation of Cuba. A day after the defeat, Kennedy met with the Miami-based Cuban Revolutionary Council. The following day he commented to Richard Nixon, whom he had summoned to his office, "They are mad. . . . Things just calmed down today and, believe it or not, they're ready to continue and fight again, if we give them the plan and the resources. . ."[22] Nevertheless, the Cuban exiles who did not participate in the invasion took a different view: Miami was incredulous and agitated. The CIA men were inconsolable.

New perspectives: The Taylor report and the Alliance for Progress

On April 23, 1961, Kennedy decided to create an inter-departmental commission to investigate the causes of the failure of

---

[21] Tripartite Conference (USA-Soviet Union-Cuba) on the Missile Crisis. Closing speech of President Fidel Castro. Havana. January 1992.
[22] Nixon, Richard. *Memoirs*. New York. Grosset and Dunlap. 1978.

the invasion and to formulate appropriate proposals. The commission would be presided over by General Maxwell Taylor, one of his military advisers. After various interviews with participants in the episode, Taylor finished his report on June 13.

The document reviewed the causes of the fiasco in terms of military and paramilitary actions, and its principal political argument changed the traditional focus on the Cuban problem. It proposed that Cuba not be confronted in isolation, but rather in the context of the Cold War. It considered two alternatives: coexist with Cuba and accept it as a reality, or include it in the government program against international communism.

Recommendation number six of the report concludes: "We concur in thinking that we cannot live for a long time with Castro as our neighbor. . . . His presence continues to be an effective exponent of communism and anti-Americanism within the community of the hemisphere and constitutes a real threat capable of toppling elected governments in any or in the majority of the weak Latin American republics. There are only two ways of looking at these threats: wait until time and internal discontent finally exterminate them, or take effective measures to force their removal. If it weren't for the time this would take, perhaps a few years more, there are a few small reasons to believe that the first form of action might be effective in Castro's police state. . . . The second has already been made more difficult by the April fiasco, and now can only be possible through open U.S. participation, with all the Latin American support that can be obtained. Neither alternative is attractive, but the first could be opted for without having to make a decision. . . . Although we are personally inclined to a position of positive action against Castro, we recognize the danger of treating the Cuban problem outside of the context of the situation of the Cold War. . . . It is recommended that the Cuban situation be reevaluated in the light of all presently known factors and that new guidelines be drawn up for propagandistic, economic, military and political action. . ."

General Taylor advised the President to radically reorganize his government and to reevaluate the emergency military powers within the framework of the balance of forces between the socialist and capitalist blocs.

Beyond U.S. frontiers, discontent was growing in Latin America. On official visits, representatives of the Kennedy administration — George McGovern and Arthur Schlesinger — had held talks in Brazil with both President-elect Janios Cuadros and outgoing President Juscelino Kubitschek, and in Argentina with President Arturo Frondizi, who confirmed the explosive situation in the region. Aware of the facts, President Kennedy resolved to project a new image toward the continent, in order to challenge the conventional wisdom that the United States was responsible for all of the social problems of the region. The best example of this new perspective was the creation of the Alliance for Progress in Punta del Este in August 1961, four months after the Bay of Pigs fiasco. The Alliance for Progress was a broad program of reforms to stimulate Latin American socioeconomic development in coordination with U.S. interests. Kennedy understood, with foresight and objectivity, the historical character of the 1960s.

In 1958, when Kennedy was a senator and a member of the subcommittee on issues affecting the American continents, this group promoted studies of the region and the need to establish criteria for the relations between the United States and Latin America. Its conclusions were brought to President Kennedy at the White House, serving as a basis for the creation of the Alliance for Progress project. Twenty countries signed the Alliance plan in Punta del Este, all except Cuba. It proposed a 10 year plan for the Americas, establishing commitments to promote capitalism, among them: a better distribution of national revenue, the diversification of economic structures, the broadening of internal markets, the acceleration of industrialization including capital assets, an agrarian reform to replace the *latifundios* and subsistence farms with an equitable system of property ownership with credit and technical assistance, the elimination of illiteracy, birth control, the development of democratic political institutions, a minimum of six years of education for all school age children, and ways of increasing the job market and the housing market, along with other social and cooperative programs.

At the time, President Kennedy declared, "Now we have to take some preventative measures. . . . [B]ut we will apply pragmatic words to our own interests. The opportunity has been given to us at this moment." Kennedy advocated a more free, just and rational treatment of foreign investments by private U.S. companies, and working together with the Latin American economies as a "partner in society," arguing that in this way each one of them in the future would be able to govern autonomously. "If we cannot help the many who are poor," he observed, "we cannot save the few who are rich." It was the premise of the Alliance for Progress that the investment of capital, education, agrarian reform and democratic development were the essential pillars for the creation of a modern state with economic and social justice.

The Kennedy initiative gave birth to a current of reformist thought in the United States and in Latin America. It assumed changing the old links established by Washington with the oligarchies of the hemisphere, through the implantation of a capitalism more acceptable to the peoples of Latin America in order to avoid a radical and revolutionary political confrontation. The proponents of this new Good Neighbor Policy on John F. Kennedy's team included historians Ted Sorensen and Arthur Schlesinger, economist John Kenneth Galbraith, foreign political adviser Richard Goodwin, and social affairs expert Richard Boone.

The Kennedy team was aware that the proposed changes were based on a process of Latin American social emancipation. In a report entitled "The Alliance for Progress: Symbol and Substance" (U.S. Senate, May 1966), Robert Kennedy reflected: "There cannot be democracy, justice or individual dignity without revolutionary changes in the economic, social and political systems of each and every one of the Latin American nations. The revolution will come, whether we like it or not. We can affect its character, but we cannot alter its inevitability. . . . It is not only an affront to our conscience that Latin Americans feel so oppressed and desperate, but also our own interests are compromised. If we don't show some preoccupation for these dispossessed people, they will rise up in revolution until they shake the foundations of our own peace and security. . . ." He added, "We were satisfied with, accepted and even backed any government, asking only that it did not disturb the superficial calm of the hemisphere. We gave medals to dictators, praised reactionary regimes and were identified with men and institutions that brought poverty and fear to their lands. . . . Anti-Americanism flourished and so did the growth of communism. Our Vice-President [he was referring to Nixon] was insulted and stoned in Caracas. . ." Two years after he made this speech, Robert Kennedy was assassinated in the United States.

Theoretically, the Alliance for Progress denounced military coups in Latin America, many of them organized by the Pentagon, and proposed a dialogue with the political ruling classes of the region in order to guarantee a peaceful climate for investment. The Alliance for Progress earned the antipathy of the region's oligarchies and the monopolies. It was a strategy of seduction, not confrontation; persuasion, not coercion.

Patty, Liborio and Peter Pan

At the same time, in the period between May and November 1961, independently of the past problems and the progress of the Taylor Report, the CIA pursued two large covert warfare operations, in the hope of improving the Agency's image in Kennedy's eyes and reorganizing its cadres. The first began at the end of May and was called Operation Patty. (It was called Operación Candela in Cuba.) The second, called Operation Liborio, got underway in the months of August and September.

Patty sought to assassinate the Castro brothers on July 26, 1961, on the anniversary of the revolutionary movement; one in Havana, and the other in Santiago de Cuba. These objectives were tied to a plan to attack the base at Guantánamo, a revival of the old project. The counterrevolutionary leaders were sheltered under the protection of the intelligence service on the base, and they dealt with the CIA through Higinio "Nino" Díaz. Agents and arms shipments had been introduced into various points in the country. Other counterrevolutionary groups had committed themselves to carrying out acts of subversion and sabotage and to assassinate local leaders. The plan was the same as always: once the two Cuban leaders had been eliminated, create chaos so that each government would believe that they were the victims of an aggression.

The principal head of the operation was Alfredo Izaguirre de la Riva, who had been recruited by the CIA in Cuba in early 1959 and who had participated in the placing of microphones in all of the places where it was thought that the Chinese and Soviet embassies might be located. He traveled illegally to Florida on various occasions. In mid May 1961 he was again chosen to go to Miami where he found a scene reeling from the aftermath of the Bay of Pigs.[23] He talked with Howard Hunt and Jack Engler, but they offered him no concrete information. Izaguirre then decided to go to Washington to contact senior Agency officials. There he was received by "Harold Bishop," (the pseudonym of a CIA official) and Frank Bender, who explained to him the situation and the existence of the Taylor Commission, investigating the failure of the Bay of Pigs invasion. They wanted to take advantage of his stay to interview him. The meeting with General Taylor took place in the offices of the Pentagon in the presence of CIA officials and functionaries of other agencies. The conversation revolved around the perspectives of the opposition in Cuba, and one of the dialogues was reproduced by Izaguirre himself: "How many men does Manuel Ray's MRP organization have?" asked one of the participants. Izaguirre responded that there were around 700. "We calculate around 200," said the interrogator. "There might be 200 or there might be 700," responded Izaguirre, "but even the combined forces of all those in the underground organizations could not defeat the Cuban government." "We agree with your evaluation, but the [anti-Castro Cubans] had better get rid of the idea that the Marines are going to intervene to solve the Cuban problem, unless you yourselves create the proper situation. . . . What possibilities exist for a general uprising on the island? An action of this nature would justify an intervention on our part. Another justification might be if the Cuban government or somebody attacked the

---

[23] According to an earlier declaration by Alfredo Izaguirre de la Riva, "Everybody cursed the Kennedy brothers and bitterly lamented the luck of the Brigade."

Guantánamo base. . . ." Under the guise of conducting an investigation, the CIA was actually passing instructions to Izaguirre. Hours later, in the intimacy of his hotel, he conveyed to Frank Bender his impressions of the meeting: "I understand that the United States needs a pretext to intervene militarily in Cuba. . . . [T]he [Guantánamo] naval base will be attacked, and you can denounce Fidel Castro as responsible for this act. . ."[24] After Izaguirre returned to Cuba, he met with his associates and explained the plans. But Cuban State Security got wind of the plot. On July 22, 1961, Izaguirre and his collaborators were arrested, their weapons confiscated and their plans frustrated.

When the CIA learned of the Patty debacle, the principal directors of the anti-Cuba operation analyzed the situation and decided to utilize the MRP (Movimiento Revolucionario del Pueblo — People's Revolutionary Movement) to salvage their people and resources in Cuba. Founded at the end of 1960 by Manuel Ray Rivero, former Minister of Public Works of the first revolutionary government, the MRP possessed a special profile. In the United States, Ray preached a social democratic line and claimed to be responsible for part of the measures taken by the revolution, such as the agrarian reform, although he condemned socialism. The MRP joined the Cuban Revolutionary Council in the months prior to the Bay of Pigs, but the principal leaders of the coalition, out of distrust tried to isolate it. Not only did the group have few links to the Bay of Pigs fiasco, but also Manuel Ray had initiated contact with Kennedy's State Department. For these reasons the MRP suited the occasion; the Taylor Report was being concluded and the CIA needed to recover lost ground with Kennedy.

In Cuba, one of the highest leaders of the MRP was Antonio Veciana Blanch, recruited in 1960 in Havana by "Maurice Bishop," (the pseudonym for a CIA official whom we mentioned earlier). In the last days of July 1961, an agent was reinfiltrated in order to contact Antonio Veciana and supply him with resources. Veciana had rented an apartment at #29 Avenida de las Misiones, on the 8th

---

[24] Declarations by CIA agent Alfredo Izaguirre de la Riva. Report on the Cuban State Security Department (G2) on "Patty-Candela" and "Liborio," 1961.

floor, approximately 70 meters in a straight line from the north terrace of the old Presidential Palace where mass meetings were held and Fidel Castro gave speeches. It was the ideal spot for an assassination attempt, for which Veciana had been oriented by "Bishop" since January. This was Operation Liborio, which had two more components: a general wave of sabotage, and Operation Peter Pan, the psychological component.

The idea for Peter Pan was developed at the end of 1960 in a meeting held in the U.S. State Department offices between Monsignor Walsh, the head of the Catholic Service Bureau of Florida, functionaries of the State Department, and CIA official "Harold Bishop." The participants agreed to unleash an operation which would spread the rumor in Cuba that parents would lose the rights of paternity over their children to the Cuban state, and that many of them would be sent to Siberia. In coordination with a highly placed Cuban cleric and James Baker, the director of the Ruston Academy in Havana, the Liborio conspirators drew up a fake "Patria Potestas" Law, to be distributed clandestinely to the population. The wave of rumors served only to launch the plan, which legalized the traffic of many Cuban children to camps in Florida. According to Monsignor Walsh's testimony, between December 1960 and October 1962, some 15,000 children left Cuba without their parents, and a large number of them never saw them again. Within Operation Liborio, this activity would create a propitious framework for Latin American nations, preoccupied with the instability of the island, to appeal to the OAS and demand a joint intervention along with the United States. But when copies of the "proposed bill" were about to be distributed, Peter Pan was denounced. One of Antonio Veciana's aides was arrested and confessed that his chief (without saying who he was and giving only his pseudonym) was involved in a very important plan and had recruited fishermen at a beach near Havana to aid him in his escape after the action. The Cuban State Security forces, in possession of other information, discovered that the operation was related to a subversive plan throughout the country and which included an attempt on Fidel Castro's life.

The president of Cuba, Osvaldo Dorticós, had left on his first trip to the socialist countries, and a mass assembly was convoked to welcome him home on October 4, 1961. Preparing for this, Antonio Veciana had brought to his apartment a U.S.-made bazooka, various machine guns, a shipment of hand grenades and revolutionary militia uniforms. He planned to assassinate Castro and then fire at random into the crowd to provoke chaos and permit the assassins, dressed as militia, to escape. On October 3 — one day before the plan was to have been executed — Veciana and other members of his group fled to the United States. The reason is not known for certain, but Veciana told investigator Gaetón Fonzi[25] that he felt that he was under suspicion after an apparently informal conversation with his cousin Guillermo Ruiz, who was a G-2 agent. The apartment and the materials inside were confiscated by Cuban State Security and on October 11, another member of the MRP was arrested on a farm on the outskirts of Havana owned by Amador Odio, who was also arrested.

Antonio Veciana Blanch, "Maurice Bishop," and Silvia Odio, one of Amador Odio's daughters, will all reappear, linked to Lee Harvey Oswald and the Kennedy assassination, in episodes which we will relate in the next chapter.

---

[25] Fonzi, Gaetón. *The last investigation*. New York. Thunder's Mouth Press, 1993. Material from the archives of the Cuban State Security Department.

CHAPTER 3

Operation Mongoose

Rumbles at the top

Months after his report on the Bay of Pigs was completed, Kennedy named General Maxwell Taylor as Chairman of the Joint Chiefs of Staff of the U.S. Armed Forces. Taylor, previously considered a military man whose career was on the decline, was quickly transformed into a powerful figure in the government. Kennedy wanted someone in that position whom he could trust, in order to keep an eye on the leaders of the Pentagon.

The selection of General Taylor increased the antagonisms. He was one of the most ardent advocates of the theory known as "limited warfare," "low-profile warfare" or "low and medium intensity conflicts," to which Kennedy was also committed. In contrast, since 1960, all of the investments and plans of the military industrial complex and the high military commands of the armed forces had been directed toward atomic weapons research, the perfection of rockets and strategic instruments of mass destruction, with a view toward employing them in a future "great war."

In the end, Taylor's viewpoint was much more practical: he defended the idea that the United States and its armed forces had to be prepared not only for a great war, but also for little wars against the revolutionary world on the rise. What seemed on the surface like little more than a difference in focus, implied a strategic change, and clashed with the views of other high ranking officers of the Pentagon.

John Kennedy also initiated a restructuring of the CIA, removing Allen Dulles as director on November 28, 1961. Dulles realized that he had become a persona non grata in the presidential circles because his access to the Oval Office had been permanently cut off. Kennedy proposed that he remain as an adviser, and named John McCone as the new director in the hope of keeping a better eye on the Agency's operations. But McCone's background, as the owner of a marine corporation, a Republican, and chairman of the Atomic Energy Commission, branded him as a real outsider in the CIA nest. Richard Bissell, assistant director of covert operations, was removed by Kennedy three months later. Richard Helms, the prominent chief of the Agency who was then serving in Eastern Europe, was summoned by Kennedy to assume that position. Before his resignation, one of Bissell's last acts was to name William Harvey to a new post: Head of Task Force W, a unit created exclusively for the purpose of carrying out anti-Cuba operations on a worldwide level, and which would function out of the CIA's central offices.

Harvey was a tall, heavyset man who, according to a member of the British Secret Service, moved around the United States wearing two pistols. An important intelligence agent since the 1950s, Harvey had been in charge of the Agency's West Berlin post until 1960, where among other things, he coordinated the episode of the famous Berlin tunnel, dug to make possible the tapping of telephone lines in Soviet military headquarters in East Berlin. The Soviets discovered the plan, and the tunnel was turned into a tourist attraction. In early 1961, Harvey was called by Bissell to head up a special project to create the means and conditions for the elimination of high political figures hostile to the United States. His work during that year consisted in studying the files and dossiers of foreigners linked to the Agency, establishing contacts with the international Mafia, recruiting cadres and familiarizing himself with related projects already carried out or in process inside or outside the CIA, such as those concerning Lumumba, Castro and Trujillo. Patrice Lumumba was assassinated in January 1961; Rafael Trujillo, in May; and plots against Castro had been in the planning stages within the CIA itself since 1959.

These facts shed a light on material uncovered in earlier investigations. The operation led by William Harvey was clearly linked to the plans to assassinate foreign leaders code named ZR-RIFLE [also known as "Executive Action"], taking as a cover the CIA's recently-created "Department of Coded Communications in Foreign Countries."

The appearance of Richard Helms and William Harvey in the context of Mongoose had another significance. Neither was tainted by any of the past Cuban operations, particularly the Bay of Pigs invasion. Their backgrounds were appropriate for the new government programs against international communism and the Soviet bloc, following the recommendations of the Taylor Report; they were officials who had been working in the special espionage services in Europe.

Mongoose

On November 30, 1961, as an express recommendation of the National Security Council and by order of President John F. Kennedy, the Special Amplified Group (SAG) was formed under the direction of Attorney General Robert Kennedy and General Maxwell Taylor. It was represented by the principal government agencies and departments including the State Department, the Undersecretary of State for Latin America, the Secretary of Defense, the Secretary of Commerce, the Pentagon, the CIA and the USIA (United States Information Agency). The SAG would become the executive board of Operation Mongoose, a new U.S. political strategy against Cuba. Why the name Mongoose? The mongoose is a carnivorous mammal of the viverrid family, native to India where it is domesticated to kill poisonous snakes, including the cobra, and devour their eggs.

Each department was charged with conceiving and executing a plan. Kennedy asked Taylor to recommend a coordinator for the project, and the latter proposed Edward Lansdale, an Air Force Brigadier General and a renowned military intelligence official. His function would be to unify the various projects. In December 1961, it was decided that the headquarters of the operation would be located in the Pentagon. On January 18, Lansdale proposed Project Cuba,[26] broken down into 32 tasks to be carried out in collaboration with the CIA's Richard Helms and William Harvey. The following day, at a meeting in Robert Kennedy's office, the SAG analyzed the project and sent it to the agencies involved for their comments. On February 20, after gathering input from the other departments, Lansdale presented an initial proposal which included distinct plans of action responding to various objectives with a timetable ranging from March to October 1962. In summary, these were the same as the earlier Cuban operations: the organization of counterrevolutionary groups on the island and abroad, international propagation of an image of instability, and finally, a military invasion. Some members of the SAG thought that the timetable was not workable. Finally, on March 11, Lansdale submitted to the SAG the "Political Guidelines of Operation Mongoose," which would be approved by President Kennedy five days later.

Apart from the preparation of the final document, the government sectors represented in the SAG had already begun taking measures in conformity with the new political orientation. The first initiative came from the Commerce Department — the imposition of a commercial embargo (the blockade) — on February 3, 1962. Walter Rostow of the Kennedy team was sent as an envoy to NATO to tell its allies that the United States would look favorably upon the governments of Western Europe if they stopped trading with Cuba. A number of European and Japanese firms, importers and exporters alike, were pressured to cut their economic ties.

The second measure came from the State Department: the expulsion of Cuba from the OAS at the meeting in Punta del Este on February 12, 1962. There is an anecdote from this meeting concerning Haiti's vote, the one lacking to reach a majority. Montevideo newspapers at the time reported that the breakfast enjoyed by the U.S. ambassador and the Haitian minister of foreign

---

[26] Official report on Operation Mongoose, February 20, 1962.

affairs was "the most expensive in the world," because the U.S. ambassador paid $5 million to the minister of foreign affairs.

Another State Department initiative was the progressive breaking of relations with Cuba by all the countries of Latin America except Mexico. Political and economic relations with Western Europe were also sabotaged.

The Defense Department also made its contribution to the assault. According to instructions in the National Security Decree No. 100, the Pentagon prepared military contingency plans with a view to a possible confrontation with its adversary. In fact, in April 1962 the U.S. military carried out a rehearsal for the invasion, dubbed "Operation Quick Kick" on the Puerto Rican coast facing Cuba, involving 83 warships, 300 airplanes and 40,000 men.

The USIA began its job of propaganda and psychological warfare, which consisted of "influencing opinion and conduct in favor of the policies and the objectives" of the United States. Radio and television broadcasts to Cuban territory were planned in September 1962. Five radio stations were installed, transmitting daily programs to various parts of the island; some of these are still in existence today.[27] Taking advantage of ocean currents in the direction of the Cuban coastline, tens of thousands of plastic bags filled with propaganda leaflets and chewing gum for children were thrown into the sea. Large quantities of children's toys decorated with propaganda slogans and U.S. flags were dropped into certain regions of Cuba. Cartoon drawings with caricatures of Fidel Castro were prepared (five million copies of these comic books were made), and conferences and seminars were held exploiting the refugee problem. Foreign dignitaries visiting the United States were taken to the camps where children were sent after leaving the island during "Operation Peter Pan," where they took photos and passed out candy and toys.

As an overall program, Operation Mongoose was the ideal plan. But from the beginning there were differences within SAG. The

---

[27] Radio Martí broadcasts daily to all parts of the Cuban territory. In 1990, TV Martí, which cost US$147 million, was able to transmit to the island for only a few minutes because Cuban electrical engineers interfered with the signal.

appointment of Lansdale as coordinator did not please some. He had been an envoy to the Philippines and Vietnam, and he was considered the great hero of the international anti-communist struggle. His "spectacular" ideas were the object of veiled criticism, and were almost always impractical. One of them, recorded in official U.S. government documents, was to line up a series of boats off the Havana shore and at midnight shine all of their lights toward the sky so that the fearful Cubans would think the apocalypse had come and then overthrow Fidel Castro. In addition, everyone involved in SAG had their own vision of the Cuban problem and considered themselves more able to direct the proposals — or with more authority to report to and be accountable to the president. Little by little, the contradictions grew sharper, although they were not over the general concepts of the project, but rather over its methods. Whether or not it was necessary to assassinate Fidel Castro was questioned by Robert McNamara and considered out of the question by John McCone, a devout Catholic. Such sustained splits are an important aspect of the formation and the division of power in the United States, a complex tapestry of diverse interests that turn antagonistic in certain circumstances. To guarantee room to maneuver and to achieve their objectives, instead of breaking with the formal balance of power, some sectors such as the Pentagon and the CIA simply create parallel or "invisible" power structures. This phenomenon is at the root of the assassination of John F. Kennedy.

The JM Wave

The President made the decision to appoint his brother Robert to supervise the activities of the Agency. On the other hand, he continued to reaffirm his policies against the Cuban regime. As a politician, he oscillated between pragmatism, morality and anti-communism. Little by little, although the effects of his stance during the Bay of Pigs invasion still prevailed, Kennedy struggled to regain support from the Cuban exile organizations. "Cuba should not be abandoned to the Communists," he declared. Behind the scenes a new secret offensive against Cuba was unfolding that would lead to the Missile Crisis of October 1962. The differences at the Mongoose headquarters did not keep the CIA from speeding up its plans.

The end of 1961. Once more Miami, Florida, was the nerve center. JM Wave was created, the code name for the CIA station behind the door reading "Zenith Technological Service." This would become one of the major bases of CIA operations in the United States. At that time the CIA consolidated the mechanisms of its invisible government that had been growing in the Miami unit since the beginning of that year. In order to better comprehend this phenomenon, it is necessary to look at how the Agency is structured in its principal center in Langley, Virginia.

In addition to the general directorate, there are three subdivisions, each with their respective director: the intelligence division, where the analysts work; the administration, which encompasses the technical services, support activities and the financing of the centers; and the operative section, which encompasses plans, special operations, covert, clandestine or parallel operations, and which is the most important, given the fact that it is in charge of all of the agents and special projects such as Task Force W and JM Wave. The deputy director in charge of special operations has the status of second in charge of the Agency, and is the person who actually directs all of the CIA centers outside the country, in spite of the fact that technically these should report to the director and possess a certain autonomy as outlined in the rules of the Agency. The guarantee of the survival of this sector is the protection it offers its sources and agents: each case, job or plan is parceled out by agents and known to only one or two operative officials, or the head of the section, depending upon its importance; but the information that the latter receives can come under the cover of agents' pseudonyms. As it moves up the hierarchy, the information is altered to protect the sources, which also permits officials to invent or cover up many things. In other words, this is the structure that ensures the plausible denial of any suspicion or accusation that might fall on the Agency.

During 1962, the heads of the Miami unit were Theodore Shackley and Gordon Campbell. JM Wave was divided into sections: maritime, which was in charge of the boats for the infiltration teams, the arms and military suppliers; communications, with sophisticated radio equipment to transmit and receive messages from the agents located in Cuba and different Florida locations; operations, which included the many infiltrated agents and counterrevolutionary organizations in Cuba and Miami where they were represented; the administration, which protected the agents' covers, acquired automobiles, rented safe houses, and paid the agents and others; and an air section for all of the transport originating in the United States, Cuba, Central America and other regions. In Miami there were 400 CIA "case officials" monitoring several thousand Cuban agents, with an annual budget of hundreds of millions of dollars. Each case official employed from four to 10 principal Cuban agents, who in turn were responsible for 10 to 30 regular agents. Any Cuban exiles who wanted to open their own businesses had only to apply to the CIA for the initial capital.

Dozens of front organizations were created or recruited: press, travel, publicity and detective agencies; arms warehouses, bars, banks, hotels, stores, print shops, real estate agencies, shipping and air lines, equipment maintenance and repair shops, research centers and other "ghost companies" to employ officials and collaborators that operated outside of the base in Miami. At its disposal were several mansions, a fleet of planes, a hundred cars and the "Third Marine Corps of the Western Hemisphere" which included hundreds of small vessels and yachts. An entire arsenal was acquired through resources originating from non-governmental sources, where it was impossible to avoid agents making deals "under the table." The companies were controlled at the level of the case official who had sufficient autonomy to run them. There were also military training camps disbursed throughout the Florida Keys, including the strangely named "No Name Key."

JM Wave was subordinate to Task Force W (under the direction of William Harvey). Together with Richard Helms, Harvey supervised activities on the Miami base, but he also drew up the policies and oriented the execution of the Cuban project for all of the Agency's foreign stations, as well as those of the CIA officials who worked in embassies of the countries where Cuba had strong diplomatic representation. Moreover, due to its size and importance, JM Wave ended up controlling the principal cases with relative independence from the central offices of the Agency, and was transformed into the international nucleus for the secret war. It also came to control the economic strategy of Mongoose, pressuring countries to cooperate in the blockade and supervising a program of sabotaging merchandise imported from or exported to Cuba. All of this demonstrated the influence on U.S. foreign policy exerted by the CIA, the magnitude of which was unknown by President Kennedy. In the case of JM Wave, the "autonomy" reached the point of having grave consequences.

Capsules — Case No. 2^{28}

When William Harvey, head of ZR-Rifle (the operation designed to eliminate political leaders), assumed control of Task Force W in November 1961, one of his first measures was reinforcing the contacts with the Mafia. Through Colonel Sheffield Edwards (head of the CIA Security Office), he established personal contact with John Roselli to propose to him the reactivation of the poison capsule plan.

The scheme was reborn with new features: now it was the clandestine operations branch itself that would execute the plans. But Harvey did not know who the agent was that had been selected by the Mafia (Tony Varona). The plan took a while to get off the ground, since it was decided to improve the product. The laboratories were asked to produce some capsules that were easier to manipulate and would dissolve in any liquid. Meanwhile, Harvey went to inspect the anti-Cuba operation in Florida.

In April 1962, the new capsules were ready, but the frequent plane trips between Miami and Havana no longer existed so Tony Varona had to rely on a CIA agent, a Spanish diplomat named Alejandro Vergara,[29] to get the capsules to Cuba. The diplomat agreed to carry them in the name of friendship. In early May,

---

[28] An account composed of excerpts of the report of the U.S. Senate Committee 1975, op. cit., and materials from the archives of the Cuban State Security Department.

[29] Vergara was subordinated to another Spanish diplomat, Jaime Capdevilla, also a CIA agent, expelled from Cuba years later for espionage activity.

Vergara, already in Cuba, got word to Alberto Cruz Caso (of "Rescate") to meet him at the Spanish Embassy and pick up the capsules. The leaders of "Rescate" immediately met to study how they could carry out the action. Since their man at the "Peking" Restaurant had already left the country, they decided to use their contacts at the Havana Libre Hotel. They went to the hotel and approached some co-conspirators who worked there. After feeling out several people, they picked maitre d's José Saceiro and Bartolomé Pérez Díaz and a bartender named Santos de la Caridad Pérez Nuñez. They explained the job: take advantage of any opportunity when Fidel Castro appeared in the cafeteria or one of the restaurants to mix the poison in his drink.

The year 1962 passed. Fidel Castro went to the Havana Libre a few times, but everything seems to indicate that the visits never coincided with the working hours of the conspirators. One of them, Santos de la Caridad, carried out a tense ritual every day when he left his house to go to work. He removed the capsules from a dresser, put them in a bag and took them to the cafeteria where he deposited them inside one of the tubes of the freezer to wait for the right moment. Almost a year passed before finally, one night in March 1963, after visiting a guest of the government who was staying at the hotel, Fidel Castro entered the cafeteria with a few other people, sat down at a table and asked the waiter for a chocolate milk shake. The barman on duty was Santos de la Caridad. Seeing the opportunity, he began nervously to go through the required motions: he got out the metal container for the blender, opened the refrigerator, poured the milk, opened the freezer, took out the chocolate ice cream and put it in the blender, and went back to get the capsules. But due to the effects of a higher refrigeration temperature that day, the capsules had frozen and they stuck to the tube. Santos de la Caridad did everything he could to get them loose, but in doing so he broke them and the poison spilled. Desperate, he had to prepare the milk shake without any further delay. Castro drank it and then went on his way, safe and sound. Another such opportunity would never reappear. The CIA would never again have the life of Fidel Castro so close to their hands.

Each of the characters in this episode would move on. On receiving the news, Tony Varona was unperturbed because when William Harvey had decided to reactivate the capsule plan, Varona was already disillusioned with it and had committed himself to others. Also, John Roselli and the Mafia leaders were transferring to Las Vegas the plans they once had for making Havana one huge casino; however, they were not happy about it because Los Vegas wasn't the shadow of that island paradise in the Caribbean.

Varona continued as a CIA agent and as an important member of Trafficante's "family." As for the leaders of "Rescate," each one of them was already setting up their own network, according to the new directions of the Agency to divert the attention of Cuban State Security. One of these networks was made up of the three employees of the Havana Libre Hotel: Santos de la Caridad, Bartolomé and Saceiro. These networks were dismantled at the end of 1964. Their members were arrested and they made statements. That was how Cuban intelligence was able to get to the bottom of the story of the poison capsules. Santos de la Caridad spent several years in jail and then moved to Miami.

The special missions

In the first half of 1962, Richard Helms and William Harvey worked out a strategy to be applied by Task Force W inside Cuba, which required the successive infiltration of agents on special missions.

One of the first to arrive was Juan Manuel Guillot Castellanos on January 14. Guillot was with the MRR, Manuel Artime's organization, although at that time Artime was in prison in Cuba, where he had been since the Bay of Pigs expedition. Remember that Artime was the political leader preferred by the officials Howard Hunt and David Phillips; and also that the MRR was one of the most powerful groups in Cuba, because it was supported by the lay organizations of the Catholic Church: the Young Catholic Students (JEC), the Young Catholic University Students (JUC), and the Young Catholic Workers (JOC).

In Havana, Guillot began working to reform the counter-revolutionary groups, beginning with the MRR. His contacts included the MRP, the November 30 group, the Christian Democratic Movement, and the Revolutionary Student Directorate. For the purpose of attracting followers, the latter borrowed the name of a strong student organization which played a part in the Cuban revolution. Guillot told them that the CIA was preparing for a large-scale operation, and that it was necessary to form a united front which would lead to an internal uprising. He then ran up against the persistent contradictions among the groups and decided to return to Florida on March 29, where he related the difficulties in reaching agreements, and proposed that the CIA remove some of the leaders in order to facilitate compliance.

In the month of April, the heads of the CIA in charge of the Cuban case formulated an offensive strategy for the uprising and decided that the following month they should infiltrate most of their "political action" agents together with shipments of arms and explosives. Financial resources for the operation also began to arrive, often through the diplomatic pouches of some European embassies where the CIA had recruited diplomats.

Guillot returned to Cuba on May 1, and was arrested on May 29, along with other agents, enabling Cuba to learn the details of the plan: terrorist activities and the occupation of various cities, air drops of military supplies into the mountainous areas, and attacks on specific coastal locations by detachments trained in Florida and Central America. In the Florida Keys, the training of these cells was carried out by Frank Sturgis and Pedro Luís Díaz Lanz's International Anti-Communist Brigades with the participation of former U.S. Marines. Since the previous year, they had been carrying out various air attacks and acts of sabotage in Cuba, which they intensified during the following period.

Fragments of testimony of persons detained by the Cuban G-2 also provided an outline of the Mongoose plan and the preparation of a second invasion.

July was a decisive month. A FAL (Anti-Communist Liberation Forces) coalition — comprising the Second Escambray Front, the DRE and the MRP — proposed to other groups the idea of a general uprising in the country; an act that presented a real threat to the revolution, not only because it indicated the existence of a united front, but also because the leaders had infiltrated men in some military and police units. One plan was drawn up by the FAL, to be carried out on August 30. It consisted of the takeover of various military, police and naval units of the capital, followed by an attack on civilian targets throughout the country with the support of cells which operated in the central zone. These actions were to have been preceded by the sabotage of electrical systems and a great barrage of propaganda. Some leaders and their representatives in exile doubted that the operation would be successful, while others were confident at least about the surprise factor, which they felt would guarantee destabilization in Havana for hours or perhaps days.

The CIA was encouraging them and closely watching the plans for the imminent rebellion in Cuba. The CIA chiefs in Washington decided to communicate their plans to General Lansdale, coordinator of the Mongoose operation. Lansdale proposed that the SAG meet in Washington with Robert McNamara (the Secretary of Defense), along with General Benjamin Harris (of the Pentagon), Edwin Martin (Assistant Secretary of State for Inter-American Affairs), Robert Kennedy, and Maxwell Taylor, to analyze the results and the perspectives of Mongoose.

Lansdale gave private instructions to Benjamin Harris to prepare a contingency plan for an eventual invasion of Cuba, assuring him that the situation provoked by the uprising would justify the military intervention. On July 25, a report was delivered to the SAG which detailed the CIA's success in Cuba in the infiltration of agents, the placing of arms, and the preparation for an intervention on August 30.

In conclusion, Lansdale offered four options for the group's approval: The first (A), suggested cancelling the operation and treating Cuba as a member of the Communist bloc. The second (B), proposed exerting all possible pressure — diplomatic, economic, psychological, etc. — to topple Castro's communist regime without the open involvement of the United States military. The third (C), was a commitment to help the Cuban groups liquidate Castro by stages, step by step, to assure success, and included the use of U.S. military forces as a last resort. The fourth (D), was to make use of a provocation and use the U.S. armed forces to eliminate the Castro government.

In simple terms, the alternatives could be reduced to three and summed up as follows: accept Cuba as a reality in the hemisphere and continue the blockade (economic strangulation) without military aggression; or turn over the responsibility for the Cuban project to the CIA so that their covert war operations and internal subversion could bring down the island's government; or organize a military invasion. Coexistence with Cuba was not acceptable. Option B was approved, but called "B amplified," meaning that once Cuban governmental power was destabilized the invasion would be justified. (Therefore, B amplified = B + C + D).[30] At the end of July the Pentagon concluded the "Contingency Plan Against Cuba."

From August 11 on, the CIA unit in Miami received more detailed information on the planned uprising and began to send this information on to Washington. At a meeting which took place in Cuba on August 17, the four coordinators of the coalition reaffirmed their willingness to attack on the set date. Some groups, such as the MRR, confirmed their support, but others, such as the November 30 Movement and Revolutionary Unity, were still afraid to join in so as not to risk another fiasco. Bernardo Alvarez Perdomo, coordinator of Revolutionary Unity, relayed to the Miami unit the results of the meeting. After analyzing the data supplied by Alvarez Perdomo, the Agency operatives in charge of the matter asked that plans be put off until September, judging that they had been hasty.

Cuban State Security had had indications of the coming invasion since the end of July, but they decided not to act. They needed more time and more information. On the evening of August 29, having no alternative, they acted to neutralize the plan, although they did not destroy its structure. Meanwhile, the CIA continued

---

[30] The approval of this option was confirmed by the National Security Council Memorandum No. 181, signed on August 23, 1962. It should be noted that General Lansdale's report was not among the documents on Operation Mongoose "declassified" by the United States in 1988, but the Cuban State Security Department was aware of its contents.

to give instructions to all of the networks to be at their posts until the order was given for the uprising following the assassination of Fidel Castro in Revolution Square or on the steps of the university. The time was pressing. According to the Mongoose timetable, October was the month for the military invasion, now backed up by the "B amplified option." Frequent infiltrations of agents and arms continued along with counterrevolutionary activities on Cuban soil, but in the month that followed the principal groups in the capital were wiped out, and their arsenals were confiscated.

Events rapidly escalated. In August and September, CIA operatives in Miami, together with William Harvey and with the approval of Richard Helms, made the decision to organize a secret "parallel" structure to direct terrorist groups. In the future this structure would become the invisible operational arm of the CIA. Men were being trained in 14 different bases in the Caribbean (in Guatemala, Nicaragua, Panama, Haiti and the Dominican Republic). Alpha 66, founded by Antonio Veciana (head of Operation Liborio), launched pirate attacks not only on Cuban and foreign vessels but also against targets on Cuban soil. On September 1 the port of Caibarién was attacked, causing both the destruction of human life and property.

There was pressure from all sides. On September 3, U.S. soldiers from the Guantánamo Naval Base shot at Cuban positions. Three U.S. senators asked the United States to sponsor a military organization among the American nations, similar to NATO, in order to deal with the problem of Cuba. The Foreign Relations Commission and the Armed Services Committee of the U.S. Senate approved a resolution on the use of troops to resist "Communist Aggression" in the hemisphere. At the beginning of October, the Congress released a joint declaration to "impede by any means the Cuban regime from forcefully extending its aggressive or subversive activities." The Defense Department announced the recruitment of Cuban refugees who wished to volunteer for special Spanish-speaking units in the U.S. Army and Marine Corps.

At the end of December, the State Department held a closed-door meeting at which they outlined measures to force the Latin American governments to turn against Cuba. Afterward, they pressured 16 countries into politically and economically isolating the island nation. From the middle of September through the beginning of October, U.S. military planes violated Cuban air space and flew over Cuban merchant marine ships as well. The United States convoked a Hemispheric Conference in the UN, for the purpose of ridding Cuba of its "Soviet communist influence." Adlai Stevenson, the head of the U.S. delegation, declared that his government reserved the right to intervene in the island. On October 4, the U.S. government accused the Cuban government of interfering in the internal affairs of Argentina, declaring that documents had been stolen in Buenos Aires on behalf of the Cuban Embassy there, although the Argentinians contradicted the accusation.

On the eve of the Missile Crisis, the theme of the subsequent part of this chapter, the CIA ordered the terrorist groups to attack points in Cuba, already aware of the existence of Soviet missiles in that country. On October 10, Alpha 66 units were close to the Havana coast. On October 20, the *Vilaro*, a large CIA vessel, arrived at the Pinar del Río coastline (west of Havana) and two teams disembarked, one of them under the command of Miguel Angel Orozco Crespo (head of special missions), with the objective of blowing up the large copper mines located in an area of this province called "Matahambre." After the Missile Crisis began, only some of the infiltrators could get back to the vessel. One of those who stayed behind was Orozco Crespo, who was arrested in early November. One of his principal revelations concerned a top secret operation: Cuban "mercenaries" were planning to attack Puerto Cabezas in Nicaragua, with the consent of President Somoza, to feign a reprisal by the Cuban government for the collaboration of the Nicaraguan dictator in the plans for the Bay of Pigs invasion. The tension created between the two countries, along with the establishment of a Cuban counterrevolutionary government on Cayo Romano (in the north of Camagüey Province) would be the pretext needed for U.S. aggression. In this way the Cuban government learned that Task Force W strategies, as demonstrated, were not only to stir up an internal revolt, but also to create an international confrontation so that Cuba could be invaded.

What was Khrushchev's "hidden motive"?

In October, the final adventures of Mongoose coincided with the unfolding of the Missile Crisis. Although it was not a "covert operation" in the classic sense, the sending to Cuba of the missiles did contain a secret that could not only have provided a viable pretext for the invasion of Cuba, but also could have provoked a nuclear war. Was this one of the ironies of history?

The October crisis has always been seen as a conflict between the two major world powers which reached a peaceful resolution through the diplomatic skills of Kennedy and Khrushchev. The silence of historians on the subject has left fertile ground for speculation about the judgements made by the leaders of the Cuban government at the time, and for accusations that President Fidel Castro was responsible for the risk to humanity of unleashing the first nuclear crisis in history.[31]

In fact, Cuba was on the margin of the negotiating table; its right to express its views was never recognized, even though it was the nation directly involved and the one that would have been most affected by a possible war. This was only settled three decades later, in January 1992, at a forum held in Havana. "The Tripartite Conference on the Crisis" — with the participation of the United States, the Soviet Union and Cuba — was sponsored by Brown University and other U.S. institutions and provided the opportunity for Cuban points of view to be made known and discussed in the presence of well-known researchers and participants of the era.

In 1961 and 1962, although he intended to negotiate an end to the arms race with the United States, Khrushchev publicly encouraged the installation of missiles in Cuba after the Bay of Pigs invasion. Fidel Castro made no comment. He believed that the Cuban people should rely on their own capacity for struggle without external assistance. On May 29, 1962, Marshal Biryuzov (code name "Petrov") arrived in Cuba, accompanied by Rashilov, the secretary of the Soviet Communist Party in Uzbekistan, in

---

[31] Doctoral thesis of Gloria María León Rojas. History Department, University of Havana, 1990.

order to present proposals on the missiles to Fidel Castro. But he didn't bring up the subject immediately. The marshal was afraid that Cuba would not accept. He first reflected on the international situation, and at one point in the conversation asked Fidel Castro if hypothetically the installation of missiles might prevent a U.S. invasion. President Fidel Castro responded, "Well, if the United States knew that this would mean a war with the Soviet Union, it would be the best way to avoid it."

The Cubans asked what kind of missiles and how many, and were told that there would be 42 medium-range missiles, of which 36 were operational. They asked for time to analyze the proposal, and called a meeting of the revolutionary leadership. The answer followed: If it would strengthen the socialist camp and at the same time contribute to the defense of Cuba, they would agree to all the missiles that might be necessary. After a verbal agreement, the agreements began to be fulfilled. The Soviet Union drew up a plan and submitted it to Cuba. Nothing was mentioned about the question of strategic arms; it said that the armed forces would send troops to reinforce Cuba's defense against the external threat and as a contribution to world peace. Everything was in line with the norms of international law.

A protocol was signed in Moscow during the first days of July 1962 by Raúl Castro, the Cuban Minister of the Armed Forces, and Malinovsky, the Soviet Defense Minister.

The missiles were installed within 76 days, and measures were taken to keep the operation a secret. Nevertheless, in August, with so many people involved in the complex installation of the bases (close to a thousand people already knew the secret), some people suspected that something strange was going on, given the conspicuous nature of the enormous trucks. But few could imagine that they contained missiles. In addition, although there was secrecy about the operation, it was still necessary to communicate about it. Some of this got back to Kennedy, who immediately wanted to know the nature of the arms — if they were offensive or defensive. Khrushchev entered the game, diverting the conversation. The Cubans, on their part, insisted on publishing the military accord. When they were questioned they never denied the strategic nature of the weapons, and they defended their right to decide for themselves what was needed for their defense. Khrushchev finally convinced Kennedy that Moscow was not going to send strategic arms to Cuba. Khrushchev, thinking that he was acting wisely, lied without considering that the missiles might be discovered. He also wanted to avoid creating a crisis for Kennedy just before Congressional elections were to be held.

But the sorcerer ended up being caught in his own spell. On October 14 the CIA confirmed the presence of Soviet missiles in Cuba: a U-2 spy plane photographed the San Cristóbal base in Pinar del Río, where some R-12's were located. Ray Cline, then deputy director of the Intelligence Division (Analysis) of the CIA, recalled three decades later, "The CIA had taken photographs of missile sites in San Cristóbal. . . . Later, others [elsewhere]. . . . My chief, John McCone, said that this was only preliminary, that he wanted proof. On October 14 it was decided to fly over with a U-2 to see if they were really there. I sent the photos to John and Robert Kennedy on October 16."[32] In fact, U.S. military intelligence had already made an investigation and informed the CIA. In mid-September they received the first information about the MRBM's and IRBM's (medium and intermediate-range ballistic missiles), and by the end of the same month they came to the conclusion that the MRBM's were in the San Cristóbal area.

After receiving the official CIA communique, President Kennedy waited six more days before making a public pronouncement, portraying himself as having been gravely betrayed. He imposed a naval blockade of Cuba, demanding the withdrawal of the missiles and strategic weapons. The United States began to apply pressure. U.S. aircraft began to patrol the region and Cubans mobilized all of their forces to resist any surprise attacks on the installations. Soviet ships arrived at the island with more missiles and were forced to return. It was the razor's edge: a justification for a military invasion fell on a silver platter into the

---

[32] Tripartite Conference (USA-Soviet Union-Cuba) on the Missile Crisis. Speech by Ray Cline. Havana. January 1992.

hands of the United States. The secret turned into a trap, placing the Cubans at a practical and political disadvantage.

On October 23, Fidel Castro received a message from Khrushchev, full of combative vigor: "The Soviet government considers the interventions as an incredible interference in the internal affairs of Cuba and provocation of the USSR. . . . Cuba can decide what it will do. . . . We reject the demands for arms control. . . . Instructions were given to the Soviet military in Cuba to be prepared for combat." The low-flying airplanes continued making daily morning flights. There was a full-blown crisis and, according to the minutes of the National Security Council of the United States, the hawks wanted to launch massive surprise bombing raids on Cuba and annihilate it.

On October 26, the Cubans met with Soviet military officials. That same day, without consulting the Cubans, Khrushchev proposed to Kennedy an agreement for the withdrawal of the missiles. On October 27, a U-2 plane flying over the north of Oriente Province was shot down, but when Cuba learned of the commencement of negotiations, it agreed to a ceasefire. The low-flying planes stopped. On October 28, the Prime Minister of the Soviet Union accepted the U.S. President's proposals on the condition that Cuba would not be the object of any aggression by the United States. On October 29, Fidel Castro proposed an additional five points, to be added to the accord, as a guarantee that there would be no invasion: an end to the economic blockade, an end to the aggressions, an end to the fly-overs and air and maritime space violations, an end to the pirate attacks, and the return of the naval base at Guantánamo. These five points were never considered, and the accord was concluded, requiring the removal of the missiles and an inspection of Cuban territory. Kennedy toughened his stand.

Indignant at the way things were developing, Cuba also assumed an intransigent position and opposed the inspection. On October 30, U Thant, Secretary-General of the UN, arrived in the Cuban capital with a peace offer: "negotiations and no inspections." He recognized that "sovereignty is a basic prerequisite," and that an aggression against Cuba would be "the end of the United Nations."

Only partial agreement was reached and the promises made by Kennedy and Khrushchev did not appear in the final text, only in the letters exchanged earlier between the two leaders. On November 15, Kennedy wrote Khrushchev that Castro wanted war. On November 20, the U.S. President announced the suspension of the naval blockade, but reaffirmed that he would maintain political and economic measures against Cuba. In the following days, when the last missiles were withdrawn, more U.S. fly-overs occurred in Cuban air space. The Cubans thought an attack was coming, but the flights were only aimed at intimidation.

Commenting on the events that led to the decision to accept the missiles, Fidel Castro later recalled: "We never considered that the missiles would be used against the United States without justification or as a first strike; nor would we have approved the arrival of the missiles if they were only for our defense. This was a secondary issue. . . . They were not essential. A military pact could have meant that an aggression against Cuba would have been equivalent to an aggression against the USSR. . . . From the first moment we saw that there was a strategy: improve the correlation of forces in the socialist camp. . . . [T]here were political, moral and ideological duties. . . . We didn't think about our problems and the possible criticism that could follow, damaging the image of the revolution in Latin America, transforming us into a Soviet military base. . . . There was a political cost: we were not unaware that the presence of the missiles would create a lot of tension."[33]

In April 1963, somewhere in Sabidowa, near Moscow, Khrushchev read to Fidel Castro the letters sent to him by Kennedy. "We have complied with all of our commitments. We withdrew the missiles from Italy and Turkey." Castro was surprised. On October 27, 1962, he had learned from Radio Moscow the terms of the agreement between Kennedy and Khrushchev, among them the removal of the U.S. missiles located in Turkey. Now the Cuban President confirmed the importance of this information, and he also heard Italy mentioned for the first time as an object of the accords. He thus realized Khrushchev's

---

[33] Ibid. Closing speech of President Fidel Castro.

"hidden motive" when he had proposed the location of missiles in Cuba. In fact, in 1962, with his customary astuteness, the Soviet leader had presented the issue within a global strategy to balance the forces between the United States and the socialist camp; but the need to accelerate the negotiations for the withdrawal of U.S. missiles placed secretly in Italy and in Turkey at the service of NATO, could well have been his immediate objective. Khrushchev also knew the true nuclear potential at his disposal, but having planted 42 missiles in Cuban territory, it would be likely that the United States would imagine that the Soviets had many more. The United States could have never imagined that he had used up all of his cards in one play.

Secret formula, the formula of deception. Neither Kennedy nor the Cubans had the correct information about the quantity of Soviet missiles. On this subject, Ray Cline pointed out, "The photographs obtained from Soviet air space made the United States estimate that they could be secured. . . . At the time of the Cuban Missile Crisis we calculated that they possessed 50 missiles, and that the United States was more advanced. . . . We convinced Kennedy that he had the superiority, but he never imagined that the General Secretary of the Soviet Communist Party would locate missiles in Cuba, and he expressed in public that if this occurred it would lead to a confrontation. . ." Castro observed at the same 1992 conference that, "In light of the facts now known about the real correlation of forces at that stage, we would have advised prudence. Nikita was a scoundrel, but I don't think he wanted to provoke a war, much less a nuclear war. He lived with the obsession of parity."

Robert McNamara, Secretary of Defense during the Kennedy administration, was the one who best defined the concept of parity or balance of power. For him the balance of power is strategic, not measured by quantity; and it exists when you have the capacity to respond, from the moment in which one can attack and the other respond with even one nuclear missile. This could cause as much destruction to humanity as those launched in greater numbers or the result of greater technology. In this sense McNamara considered that parity already existed prior to October 1962, and for him the transfer of missiles to Cuba did not alter the strategic balance.

"There was a great inequality in the figures," he later noted. "I calculated that the Soviet Union had a little more than 3,000 nuclear warheads. . . . We had 5,000. . . . But neither Kennedy nor I felt that we had the first strike capacity, neither before nor during the crisis. . . . We felt that we were deterring the Soviets, not provoking them. . ."[34] Any nuclear attack was unthinkable, at least for Kennedy's group, which was not prepared to pay such a high price in the face of a world opinion which was already showing signs of discontent with the arms race and the Cold War.

Not only McNamara, but all of the U.S. authorities and Kennedy collaborators at that time affirmed that they were not going to invade Cuba, independent of the crisis or its consequences. But there were contingency plans and the covert actions of Mongoose which projected a direct invasion. One of the Cuban specialists participating in the 1992 tripartite meeting questioned Kennedy's Secretary of Defense in that regard: "Did you have contingency plans for invading Cuba?" McNamara responded affirmatively, with the justification that such plans are always made by the army to confront potential enemies. The Cuban observed: "We never made contingency plans against you. And you are not our potential enemies, but rather our real enemies. . ." He continued, "And if a bombardment of the Guantánamo Naval Base would have been provoked?" McNamara hesitated: "Well. . . ." and the other continued, "Why, if you were capable of blowing up a boat [the *Maine*] here in Havana Bay and killing your own soldiers in order to enter into the Cuban-Spanish war, why wouldn't you have fired on this military base, which has no importance?"

At another point, the former Secretary of Defense admitted: "I want to be honest. If I were a Cuban, I would have thought the same way. We could have invaded."

---

[34] Ibid. Speech by Robert McNamara.

CHAPTER 4

Mysteries in the cards

Crossed lines

In January 1963, when Operation Mongoose was officially deactivated, General Lansdale wrote a memorandum addressed to the Undersecretary of State for Latin America, declaring that the operation would be "discontinued" and asking that all the documents be filed away in the archives.

The dismantling of Mongoose was part of a redefinition of Kennedy's policies toward Cuba. The President recommended to McGeorge Bundy that a new special group be constituted within the National Security Council to reconsider the Cuban question. The Executive Committee of the National Security Council issued guidelines to different government agencies and bureaus, so that, given the political and military successes uncovered after Operation Mongoose and the Cuban Missile Crisis, they might formulate new proposals. In April 1963, McGeorge Bundy (National Security Adviser) gave the National Security Council a memorandum offering various alternatives, among them "moving in the direction of the gradual development of some kind of agreement with Castro." In the first days of June the members of the Executive Committee agreed that it would be "a useful task to determine if it is possible to create channels of communication with Castro." This new strategy, named "constructive alternatives" by Bundy, represented one of the options that the Kennedy brothers, distrustful of the CIA and the Cuban exiles, would employ in the second half of 1963.

On the other hand, in the middle of June, a program of subversive activities approved by Kennedy was already being unleashed against Cuba. It was composed of three large operations, including the destruction of the principal oil refineries, some electrical power plants, and one of the most important Cuban sugar mills, the "Brazil." Along with this, the United States government planned to strengthen the economic and political blockade and the activities of psychological warfare and deceit within the island in such a way that the Cuban authorities would find themselves compelled to adopt the direction outlined by McGeorge Bundy.

In September of that year, on the initiative of William Attwood (special adviser to the United States delegation to the United Nations) and with the explicit support of Bundy, President Kennedy approved the following feeler, to be sent to the Cuban government through Carlos Lechuga (head of the Cuban Mission to the UN): whether or not Fidel Castro was willing to negotiate the conflict between the two countries. Kennedy insisted that Attwood make it clear "that it was not the United States which sought to establish the dialogue." Relations with the Soviet Union were a strong determining force behind this initiative: Kennedy's advisers — prominent graduates of Harvard University — had sensed the contradictions which arose between Cuba and the Soviet Union during the Missile Crisis, when the Cuban positions were not considered, and they argued that certain forces inside Cuba had begun to waver on the path of socialism.

For all these reasons it can be argued that the Kennedy administration was developing a dual strategy in relation to Cuba: at the same time that they put into effect the blockade and other measures to neutralize the influence of the Cuban revolutionary movement on Latin America, they were also trying to separate Castro from the Soviet orbit.

On the part of the CIA we will find old and new practices and contradictory paths. During the first half of 1963 the Special Missions Group reorganized with a new form and name: the Commandos. Mercenary forces were being trained in Central

America and Fort Jackson and Fort Benning (in the United States), composed mainly of members of "Brigade 2506" (the Bay of Pigs), with the goal of serving as the vanguard for U.S. troops in an eventual invasion of Cuba. In January 1963, William Harvey was appointed to a post in Rome. A going-away party was organized during which James Angleton held a conversation with him. Harvey, in a bitter tone and after drinking too much whiskey, accused Kennedy of being responsible for all of his misfortunes. With Harvey out of the way, Task Force W was dissolved and the SAS (Special Affairs Service) was created under the direction of Desmond FitzGerald, in search of more subtle methods to deal with the anti-Cuba cause. Such was the case that, according to the Church Commission, one of the new plans to assassinate Fidel Castro was related to scuba diving: the Cuban leader would receive special equipment for this sport impregnated with the tuberculosis bacillus. Another plan was to place explosive seashells in two places where he normally went diving. In addition, FitzGerald would also retrieve Task Force W schemes used for penetration in 1961 and 1962, this time under the name of Operation AM-LASH.

AM-LASH[35]

Behind this code name hid a potential assassin of Fidel Castro whose job it was to instigate a military coup within the revolution: Rolando Cubela. According to the investigations of the Cuban State Security Department, he had been working for the CIA since 1961.

In the late 1950s, Cubela was one of the principal leaders of the Revolutionary Directorate. This organization, together with the Popular Socialist Party (PSP) and under the leadership of Fidel Castro and the July 26 Movement, played a leading role in the overthrow of the Batista dictatorship. In 1958 Cubela joined the guerrilla movement in the province of Las Villas, where he reached the rank of commander. When the revolution triumphed on

---

[35] An account composed of excerpts from the report of the U.S. Senate Committee 1975, op. cit., and materials from the archives of the Cuban State Security Department.

January 1, 1959, he left Las Villas, advanced toward Havana and took over the Presidential Palace, the symbol of power. Cubela's connections ranged from José Antonio Echevarría, the president of the FEU (Federation of University Students), assassinated by Batista's police on March 13, 1957 (the day of the "assault on the Presidential Palace"), to the politicians of the Partido Auténtico (Authentic Party). During 1959 Cubela held various posts in the revolutionary government, including as Vice-Minister of Government. At the end of October he was elected president of the FEU, defeating Pedro Luís Boitel, the candidate supported by the Catholic hierarchy and the nascent counterrevolution. During the first part of his term as director of the FEU, he remained very active politically: he formed the University Student Militia and strengthened ties with other student organizations, primarily those in Latin America.

Rolando Cubela was a charismatic personality, egocentric and complex, with many faces. Toward the middle of 1959, José Alemán Gutiérrez, an old friend and adviser from the period of exile, arranged for him to see a psychiatrist to overcome his "identity crisis." At that time, Cubela was quite disturbed, complaining that he had not received the governmental positions he deserved. In March 1961 he went to Mexico to participate in an event in solidarity with Cuba, called by ex-president Lázaro Cárdenas, shortly before the Bay of Pigs invasion. His stay in Mexico aroused the suspicion and the criticism of Cuban diplomats who reported on the parties and drinking which took up much of his time in the capital and in Acapulco.

On that occasion his friend Carlos Tepedino (an Italian residing in Cuba and the proprietor of a jewelry store in the Havana Libre Hotel) introduced him to an American who was said to be an expert in the subject of international communism — but who was in fact an agent of the CIA — and the two held long conversations. He tried to convince him of the existence of communist elements in Cuba and to persuade him to change his position, for the purpose of creating dissension within the revolutionary movement and of recruiting him. At that point Cubela's reaction was one of doubt. He thought that the United States was overestimating the influence of the communists.

In mid-1961, Cubela was invited to another student convention in Geneva, Switzerland. Before leaving, Tepedino told him that he was also going to Europe to open another jewelry store, and that he would meet him in Rome. During the convention Cubela telephoned his friend and arranged an appointment. He spent a few days vacationing in Rome and Tepedino took advantage of the opportunity to introduce another Cuban also reputed to be a specialist in international communism. It was the CIA again, trying to complete the ideological work they had begun in Mexico. They agreed not to convert Cubela into an informant, but rather to act inside Cuba with an eye toward preventing the rise of the communists. For the same purpose Cubela also established links with the FBI through José Alemán Gutiérrez, who was connected to the Mafia in Florida. Cubela returned to his country and at the end of 1961 finished his term of office in the FEU. He rejoined the Armed Forces until mid-1962, when he asked for a leave to practice as a physician. By August he was back in Europe.

The road to Mongoose. Cubela was in Paris on an official mission. He called Tepedino in New York and told him he wanted to defect. Tepedino immediately went to meet with him; he fed his ego and tried to convince him that this was not the proper attitude, arguing the necessity to confront the revolutionary government. He calmed him down. As on other occasions, he was accompanied by an official from Langley, and little by little they worked out a plan. Cubela finally came to an agreement with the CIA, and he promised to return to Cuba and activate his collaborators to confront the policies of the revolution.

For the first time the objectives of killing Fidel Castro and carrying out a military coup were mentioned. The deadline for Operation Mongoose was October, and therefore AM-LASH became part of its global strategy. Cubela received enough money to pay all of his expenses and get his internal group moving.[36] A telegram from that official appeared in the 1975 Senate

---

[36] Cubela's group was not the DRE mentioned in the "Special Missions" clause.

investigation: it informed the CIA center of the agreement in such a way that it appeared that Cubela was the one who proposed the assassination, and recommending that he should be given some help so that he would not lose interest. The telegram was signed "Official of Case No. 1."

Upon returning to Cuba, Cubela renewed his contacts and began to work out a way of carrying out his plan, but since the actions of Operation Mongoose were cancelled and the Missile Crisis took place, the case was postponed.

The CIA was waiting patiently for another opportunity. They had infiltrated agents alongside Cubela to keep an eye on him without provoking suspicion. He was not an ordinary agent, he was a political figure with no set time for completing his tasks. Around the middle of 1963 Cubela had another depressive crisis. Taking advantage of the visit of a delegation of old student leaders to Sao Paulo and Rio de Janeiro, he left the country disillusioned: he felt that he had no future in Cuba, that the revolution there was not his revolution; that he became completely disenchanted upon learning of the Soviet missiles in Cuba; that he wanted a government not like that of Batista, but rather like that of Carlos Prío, together with the United States, where he could go to Varadero and night clubs; that this government of literacy campaigns and peasants was no longer what he wanted; that there were very few opportunities to put his plan into action. He considered himself a great leader but by 1963 he already realized that very few people supported him, that the real leader was someone else.

In Sao Paulo he telephoned Carlos Tepedino, saying once again that he was going to defect and asking him to send the fare for a ticket. By the beginning of September he was already in Paris and Tepedino set up a meeting between him and two case officials who were prepared for new sessions of "ideological psychoanalysis" in Parisian comfort. Cubela was encouraged, but he reacted aggressively at feeling pressured to follow through with the plan. He said that he could only remain in Cuba if he could have the concrete conditions to do something decisive in favor of the island and demanded the unconditional support of the United States:

"No, no I'm not an agent of the CIA, I don't admit it! I'm a friend of the United States, but in order to move forward I need to meet with a representative of the Kennedys!" Pointing out the capabilities that he lacked at the time in Cuba, he imposed other conditions: military logistics and financial resources to prepare the infrastructure of a rebellion.

One of the CIA officials told Cubela to wait while he went to Washington. He transmitted the demands to Desmond FitzGerald, who then consulted with Richard Helms. Helms told FitzGerald to go himself to Paris as the personal representative of Robert Kennedy. In October a meeting was held between Cubela and FitzGerald, who presented himself as a Democratic senator representing the Kennedys and gave the necessary assurances to proceed, saying that John, Robert and the United States government would support him. At the end of the meeting FitzGerald told Cubela: "Now, you have to discuss the other details with these two officials who are in charge of your case." He then returned to Washington. What Cubela didn't realize was that there were multiple plans in motion. FitzGerald, the head of the SAS, had included the planned assassination and coup in the global anti-Cuba operation. The man who would support him was Manuel Artime, who was in command of the groups that were training in Nicaragua.

Cubela demanded that the officials provide him with an instrument or some modern method to commit the crime and escape. He also discussed other aspects of his general program: the preparation of two guerrilla fronts in the central zone (Escambray) and in the western area (Pinar del Río), so that after carrying out the attempt he could withdraw to one of these two bases. The case officials went directly to FitzGerald. FitzGerald then requested the CIA laboratories to make a pen in whose point could be deposited a powerful poison and which would be so small that it would cause no pain if it were introduced into any part of the body. According to specialists and investigators from the Senate Committee, it could feel like a mosquito bite. The month of October passed. November came and there was still no reply. Cubela grew desperate. He had sent letters to his family saying that he was about to return, and he had reserved tickets for Havana via Prague when one of the officials returned and paid him a visit. Cubela received him with protests. The official argued that a pen was being prepared, but that it was necessary to wait a while. Cubela responded that they were delaying much more time than he had in order to return to Cuba without arousing suspicion, and that he was leaving. The scene ended as usual: Cubela was pacified.

In the sight of the hunter

While AM-LASH was being prepared, Manuel Artime returned to Florida after spending almost two years in prison in Cuba. On December 24, 1962, the 1,189 prisoners captured at the Bay of Pigs were freed and sent to Miami in exchange for U.S. compensation for the damages caused by the invasion, valued at $54 million in medicine and tinned foods.

Let us look more carefully at the consequences of the changes in the official United States policy toward the Cuban revolution, particularly in the context of the flourishing of terrorist groups. As was related in Chapter 3, since the middle of 1962 these terrorist groups had not limited themselves to attacking Cuba, but also Soviet ships and vessels of other nationalities with cargo from or for the island, and therefore the U.S. government was obliged to intervene. Among the terrorist groups which felt the governmental pressure, the most closely watched were Veciana's Alpha 66 and the former Cuban pediatrician Orlando Bosch's Insurrectional Movement for the Recovery of the Revolution (MIRR). Alpha 66 was transformed into one of the richest and most aggressive groups, and Veciana traveled constantly, looking for contacts, financing and openings for representation. MIRR already had a history of sabotage and CIA infiltration in the Escambray mountains before the Bay of Pigs invasion, receiving the support of the International Anti-Communist Brigades of Frank Sturgis and Díaz Lanz. A Puerto Rican sherriff in Florida, who had earlier collaborated in giving free reign to the groups, began to visit their camps and threaten them. Authorities of the Department of Immigration applied sanctions against them. Three camps were surprised by visits from federal and local Florida police. In February and March

1963, some camps which had previously operated openly were dismantled. In the summer of 1963, President Kennedy ordered the FBI to definitively close the camps and confiscate the weapons. "No-Name Key," the large camp in Florida, was raided by authorities. The antagonism of Miami Cubans to Kennedy intensified.

Faced with this new situation the CIA resolved to move their major groups to Nicaragua, under the leadership of Manuel Artime — their "golden boy," as he was called by counterrevolutionary leaders — although other groups remained in Florida and in the area around New Orleans. The selection of Artime also met another criteria: he was a friend of the dictator Somoza, with whom he had business dealings. Before his detention Artime had participated with Somoza in the trafficking of whiskey and drugs, with the connivance of other Latin American dictators. Arriving in Nicaragua, Artime made possible the opening of the camps, and decided that they should be set up in the area located between Bluefields and Monkey Point and in the north of Costa Rica. Below Bluefields all of the land is jungle, up to the mouth of the San Juan River, which marks the frontier between Nicaragua and Costa Rica.

The operation required absolute secrecy. One of the immediate objectives of the CIA was to train paramilitary terrorist commandos composed of men with a high level of military preparation. An organization of approximately one thousand men was created and charged with carrying out attacks along the Cuban coast and taking the Varadero Peninsula or some other zone or islet among the more than three thousand in the region. This was to coincide with Cubela's efforts at inciting his group to rebellion inside Cuba, provoking the uprising of the rest of the population, and carrying out his attempt on Fidel Castro with the poison pen. Cubela was unaware that Artime's plan was already underway.

The afternoon of November 22, 1963. In an apartment used for clandestine meetings in Paris, the deadly pen was turned over to Rolando Cubela. While details of the planned assassination were being discussed, the telephone rang. The CIA official answered. On the other end of the line the chief of the Agency's Paris office, who was not involved in the conspiracy, informed him that he had just received the news that John Kennedy had been assassinated in Dallas. He told him to sever the contact until things cleared up. In a tense manner the official turned to Cubela, told him of the death of the President and of the great concern in the country; he said that he would come back later, but Cubela objected. Besides, Cubela already had the means, the money and the plan, and he left via Prague for Havana. Case No. 1 would be reopened later.

The orchestra was playing a macabre symphony in three movements: Rolando Cubela, Manuel Artime and Lee Harvey Oswald. One part was over: President Kennedy had been assassinated.

"I am a patsy"

From the first news agency dispatches, Cuban responsibility for the assassination was insinuated. A culprit appeared very rapidly who had been in the Soviet Union and who sympathized with the Cuban revolution: Lee Harvey Oswald, 24 years old, born in New Orleans on October 18, 1939. Let us examine the detailed information transmitted by the U.S. press in those first few days, enriched by biographical information on Lee Harvey Oswald produced by U.S. researchers[37] and data supplied by the Cuban State Security Department.

His mother was a widow who moved the family to Fort Worth, where Oswald had a modest childhood. Dallas, November 23 (AP) — "During his whole life he was a loner and an introvert, he admitted without hesitation that he was a communist. . . . One policeman from Fort Worth — who asked that his name be withheld — said that he knew Oswald from the time they were both in the 5th grade until he entered high school in that city." The policeman recalled that Oswald was always opposed to any kind of discipline, seemed to have something against authority, and was never like other children who hung out together; he mentioned

---

[37] See: Garrison, Jim. *JFK: On the trail of the assassins*; Hinkel, Warren and Turner, William. *The fish is red (The history of the secret war against Castro)* New York. Harper and Row. 1981; and Fonzi, Gaetón, op. cit.

that he began to be interested in communism at age 15, "when a Marxist pamphlet fell into his hands, and later he read *Das Kapital* by Karl Marx, the Bible of Communism."

In 1956, when he was 16 years old, he abandoned his studies and joined the Marines, less than a month after having enrolled in high school in Fort Worth. In 1957, Oswald received training as a radar operator in the air base at Atsugi, Japan, the secret base for special CIA operations, from which U-2 planes set out on their spy missions and the deployment of Soviet spy planes could be detected.[38] Upon his return to the United States, Oswald was stationed at the United States Marine Base at El Toro, California, from November 1958 to September 1959, where he was a friend of Gerry Hemmings, one of the future heads of Interpen.[39] At the El Toro base he was given special treatment: he learned and practiced Russian with Naval Intelligence, although he did not need to know this for his duties as a radar operator.[40] Oswald was also trained in the Civil Air Patrol Squadron, where the chief of the "Falcons" was David Ferrie, who had a major influence on him. The Associated Press bulletin of November 22, 1963, divulged declarations by a lieutenant colonel named Curly: "In Japan [Oswald] never rose beyond the rank of private. . . . He learned Russian as part of his military training and he took his final exam two months before deserting for the USSR. . . . His military career was a failure; on two occasions he was court martialed for breaking the rules. . . . On September 11, 1959, he was granted leave to contribute to the support of his mother, and he was placed in the non-active military reserve."

---

[38] Two CIA documents quoted by the Warren Commission — CD 931 (on Oswald's access to information concerning U-2 planes) and CD 692 (a copy of an official dossier on Oswald) were "classified" as secrets. Other "unavailable" documents include the chronology and photographs of Oswald in the Soviet Union, Oswald's activities in Mexico, and a memorandum by Richard Helms entitled "Lee Harvey Oswald."

[39] The Cuban State Security Department obtained information that during 1959 Gerry Hemmings was also infiltrated into the Cuban Air Force, in the same group as Díaz Lanz and Frank Sturgis.

[40] Naval artillery information was directed by the ONI — the Office of Naval Intelligence.

A month later he was in the Soviet capital. All that is known about his trip is that he arrived in Moscow on a train from Finland on October 16, 1959. Dallas, November 22 (UPI) — "The United States Embassy confirmed today that Lee Harvey Oswald had been in Russia. An official of the Embassy said that Oswald visited the American Embassy in November 1959. . . . He added that he did not know when the suspect had visited Russia, the purpose of his trip, nor how long he stayed. . . . Unconfirmed reports said that Oswald had asked for Soviet citizenship, but could not obtain it." Another dispatch reported that on October 30, 1959, he appeared in the United States Embassy in Moscow, telling officials that he wanted to renounce his U.S. citizenship and that he was a Marxist. The Federal Bureau of Investigation confirmed that Oswald offered to tell the Soviet authorities everything he had learned while enlisted in the Marine Corps and operating radar.

After deciding to turn over military secrets, Oswald disappeared for several weeks, possibly in the custody of the KGB, the Russian intelligence. Was he granted Soviet citizenship? In Minsk he had many privileges: he worked in a radio factory and had a well-furnished apartment. At this time he had just met Marina Nicholaevna, who was employed at the City Hospital in Minsk and was the niece of a colonel in the Soviet Ministry of the Interior. They married and had one child. Had Oswald revealed secrets to the KGB? What had he told them about the base in Japan? The radar or radio frequency signals of the passing of the U-2, the "invisible" U.S. spy plane? Did the Soviets have sufficient instruments for verification? The fact is that six months after Oswald's arrival in Russia, Francis Gary Powers' U-2 was downed in Soviet territory. Powers was saved and held prisoner in the Soviet Union. With this incident, the Khrushchev-Eisenhower peace talks fell apart.

UPI, November 22 — "The assassin of President Kennedy is a confessed Marxist who spent three years in Russia trying to renounce his United States citizenship, but later changed his mind and obtained return passage to North America, paid for by the United States government. He left the USSR in 1962. . ." On November 23, the *New York Times* reported that Oswald returned to the United States after a request was made by Republican Senator John G. Tower of Texas, and thanks to a loan granted to him by the United States government. Wire dispatches added that officials of the embassy had reviewed his case, and since he had not been granted Soviet citizenship, they consented to reissue his passport. Oswald arrived in his native country in June 1962. Everything indicated that he had totally changed his ideas and would never become a Soviet propagandist. The man accused of defecting returned peacefully to the United States, without ever being tried or imprisoned. He was never censured by either Naval Intelligence or the CIA for having given away "classified" information.

A new chapter was opened in the history of Oswald. He would no longer be presented as a United States deserter, an ex-Marine, but rather as a Castro communist, as UPI dispatches related. Bulletins from November 22 indicated that Oswald was a "North American follower of Castro" or a "Marxist supporter of Cuban Prime Minister Fidel Castro."

Resuming life in America with Marina and their daughter, Oswald spent three months in Fort Worth. In October, he moved to Dallas and within a few days was already employed by the company Jagger-Stoval-Chiles (the enterprise contracted by the Pentagon to produce maps and graphs for military use), where he worked for six months. He made contact with the community of Russian immigrants there, all anti-communists, including a couple, the de Mohrenschildts, who would become good friends with Oswald and his wife in Dallas.

George de Mohrenschildt, called "the baron" by his friends, had already traveled half the world and spied for the French, the Germans, the Soviets and the Mexicans during World War II. He was well-known in Russian-American circles, and was frequently mentioned in newspaper society columns. His business was oil; he had an office in Dallas, and both he and his wife were members of the restricted Dallas Petroleum Club. Two people linked to de Mohrenschildt were George and Herman Brown, who financed the political career of Lyndon Johnson. Two years earlier in Guatemala, at the time of the training of the brigade for the Bay of

Pigs invasion, this spy disguised as an oil magnate (or vice versa) produced a long report complete with photographs for the CIA. At that time he began a geological investigation deal, and in April 1963 de Mohrenschildt went to Port-au-Prince, Haiti, to close it. The Senate Intelligence Committee in 1975 declassified a CIA security document dated April 29, 1963, which revealed that CIA agent Herbert Atkin had requested a check for de Mohrenschildt. The reasons were not clarified, but de Mohrenschildt's mission was to supervise a plot to overthrow Haitian President Papa Doc Duvalier, set for June. That month de Mohrenschildt was in Haiti. The relationship between him and Oswald was not considered by the Warren Commission, which argued that it was a curious aspect of Oswald's life. George de Mohrenschildt committed suicide in 1977, hours after a meeting with an investigator from the House Committee on Assassinations. Later a CIA agent in Dallas declared that he had asked de Mohrenschildt to keep an eye on Oswald after his return from Russia.

Dallas, November 22 (UPI) — "The police today detained Lee Harvey Oswald, identified as the president of the Fair Play for Cuba Committee [FPCC]." In May 1963 Oswald had already moved to New Orleans. At this stage various people using Oswald's name began to appear, looking for work or engaging in other activities. With the help of an ex-FBI agent, the real Oswald found work as a second lubricator in the Reilly Coffee Company, but he was never at his job. In June Oswald applied for a new passport and received one within 24 hours.[41] In July, in the middle of the summer, Oswald began "evangelizing" in the streets of New Orleans, distributing pro-Castro pamphlets stamped with the address of the FPCC — 54 Camp Street, New Orleans — located in the same block as the offices of the intelligence community. On the second floor of this corner building was the then inactive office of the old Cuban Revolutionary Council, the group of leaders of anti-Castro organizations referred to in the second chapter, who were to

---

[41] *New York Times* of November 23, 1963, affirmed that this new passport was obtained on the pretext that he was a photographer and would be traveling abroad at the end of that year.

have been the future provisional government of Cuba after the Bay of Pigs invasion. Sergio Arcacha Smith, one of the members of the CRC, was the head of this New Orleans office, but he had left for Texas a year earlier. By "coincidence" the same floor also housed Guy Banister Associates, whose director used the side entrance (531 Lafayette Street). Guy Banister was a seasoned agent who began his career in the Office of Naval Intelligence (ONI), and had been a special agent of the FBI in Chicago and also an associate of Arcacha Smith.

What was the Fair Play for Cuba Committee? It was an organization in solidarity with Cuba with branches in several U.S. cities, but it didn't exist in New Orleans until Oswald named himself the local representative, without any authorization, as part of the pro-Cuba facade that was being fabricated. On news reports that Oswald was a member or the president of the FPCC, Fidel Castro declared in a speech to the Cuban people transmitted by national television the day after Kennedy's assassination: "They say that [Oswald] appeared as the secretary of a branch of the Committee in New Orleans or Dallas; in some dispatches they say that it was in the month of August, others say that it was last week. We dedicated ourselves to the task of compiling all of the information to which we had access — statements or publications — to see if a Fair Play for Cuba Committee existed in this area of Texas or New Orleans. We searched through all our reports. The cities where there are Fair Play for Cuba Committees that we know about are New York, Los Angeles, Cleveland, Baltimore, Chicago, Tampa, Youngstown, Washington, San Francisco, Minneapolis, Philadelphia, Detroit. . . . Nowhere does anything appear about Dallas or New Orleans." [42] The national director of the Fair Play for Cuba Committee later affirmed that Lee Harvey Oswald held no post in any of the regular branches of the organization, which was later dissolved. The by-laws of the FPCC were never sent to Texas or Louisiana.

The ultra right-wing organization for which Banister worked, the Caribbean Anti-Communist League, was in permanent contact

---

[42] *Revolución*. Havana. November 24, 1963.

with the intelligence services of Anastasio Somoza and Fulgencio Batista. It was a link in the chain between the anti-communist groups and the U.S. power structure. Its members were racists and cursed Kennedy's support for Black rights; they recruited students and infiltrated U.S. universities. Since Operation Mongoose, Banister's office had been a center of arms supply and distribution frequented by a large number of Cuban exiles, Lee Harvey Oswald, Clay Shaw (director of the International Trade Mart) and David Ferrie.[43] Banister's unit was part of a line of contraband weapons that characterized the "Louisiana Corridor" (Dallas-New Orleans-Miami), controlled by the Mafia, including Jack Ruby (a Mafia leader from Dallas and the future assassin of Lee Harvey Oswald) and directed in Miami by Santos Trafficante.[44]

Where were these arms going? To the camp at Lake Pontchartrain, near New Orleans, where the International Anti-Communist Brigades and the Interpen installed their bases patterned on those they had in Florida, financed by groups of ultra conservatives and by the Mafia itself. At the camp, under the direction of Frank Sturgis and Gerry Hemmings, marksmen practiced and were trained in paramilitary operations. The majority of them were Cubans belonging to counterrevolutionary groups such as the DRE, the M-30-11 (November 30 Movement), and principally Orlando Bosch's MIRR, already mentioned in the

---

[43] Ferrie was involved very early in anti-Castro actions. He participated in the ill-fated Bay of Pigs invasion and flew planes loaded with bombs on missions paid for by Eladio del Valle, an ex-Cuban parliamentarian linked to Santos Trafficante. Shortly after the Bay of Pigs, he began to work directly with Sergio Arcacha Smith and was subsequently contracted by Guy Banister. He liked to recite anti-communist slogans for counterrevolutionary groups.

[44] Jim Garrison followed a trail that led to the contraband weapons business: a mission conducted by David Ferrie at an air base in Houma, a town in Southern Louisiana. The men entered an explosives depot of the Schlumberger Corporation, and took munitions which were then taken to New Orleans. Schlumberger was a large French company which served petroleum producers all over the world and which had supported the OAS (Secret Army Organization), a French counter-revolutionary body supported by the CIA. Clay Shaw, as well as being the director of the International Market of New Orleans, was also the director of Permindex, which financed the opposition created by the OAS to the independence of Algeria.

preceding pages. There was also a group of former U.S. pilots and soldiers, including Oswald. David Ferrie was one of the instructors.

In mid-1963, Frank Sturgis' brigade launched new attacks on oil refineries near Havana from the base at Lake Pontchartrain, as well as assaults on Soviet ships, such as those which occurred at the time of the Missile Crisis. In spite of presidential determination to close the training camps, Lake Pontchartrain continued to be treated leniently by police inspectors. In August they finally received a visit from the police and the FBI, who confiscated their weapons and explosives. This information appears on the first page of the *Times Picayune* newspaper on August 1, 1963: "Hideaway for bomb materials discovered. . . . More than a ton of dynamite, bombs 90 cm in size, napalm and other materials were confiscated Wednesday by agents of the Federal Bureau of Investigation, while an investigation was being held on the intent to carry out a military operation against a country with which the United States maintains peaceful relations."

On August 2, another news article appeared about a chalet-hideaway on the north shore of Lake Pontchartrain, where a great quantity of explosives and war materials was discovered. The wife of the owner of the chalet declared that her husband (William Jules McLaney) had loaned the house to a Cuban refugee ("José Juárez") in return for the favors of other Cuban friends. The McLaneys — William and his brother Mike — had gambling and tourist businesses in Havana in 1959, and afterwards they moved to New Orleans. In that news story, based on information supplied by the FBI, no details were mentioned about the training camp, the arrests that had been made, or about the country which was to be the target of the invasion. In fact, the FBI not only discovered arms, but also detained nine Cuban exiles and two North Americans, known as "the Pontchartrain 11," who operated in the camp and were preparing for future attacks on Cuba. One of the North Americans was Rich Lauchli, an arms dealer and founder of the Minutemen, an extreme right-wing paramilitary group; the other was Sam Benton, who had worked in Havana gambling casinos and who was an intermediary between Mafia leaders and Cuban exiles. They were all released within a few hours.

After the Kennedy assassination and in possession of literature that Oswald had distributed in the streets, U.S. Secret Service agents went to the address of the FPCC to find out if the suspect Oswald had worked there. The office was closed, but an ex-accountant revealed to them that the owners were Cubans, members of organizations known as the Crusade for Free Cuba Committee and the Cuban Revolutionary Council, and that Sergio Arcacha Smith was authorized to sign checks for both organizations. The agents returned reporting that they could find no trace of the Fair Play for Cuba Committee at that location. During the Senate Committee investigation in 1975, many witnesses testified that Guy Banister was linked to Lee Harvey Oswald. One of them was Delphine Roberts, Banister's secretary, who also said that her boss received funds from the CIA. Banister's widow also declared that it was Oswald who distributed the "Hands Off Cuba" pamphlets, the "communist propaganda" printed in the office, and that agents of the federal government took away her husband's files hours after his death in 1964. That day New Orleans police (who arrived at the office after the federal agents) found some notes referring to indexes to the folders in the files, which included: "United States Central Intelligence Agency," "Latin America," "Anti-Soviet (activities)," "Arms and Munitions," "Deactivated Missile Bases (Turkey and Italy)," "International Trade Mart," etc.

New information from the news agencies added another connection between Lee Harvey Oswald and anti-Castro Cubans. Dallas, November 22 (UPI) — "In Miami the Directorio Revolucionario Estudiantil (DRE) [Revolutionary Student Directorate], made up of young anti-Castro Cubans, confirmed that Oswald had argued about the communist gains in Cuba with a DRE representative on a radio program. According to the DRE, Oswald tried to infiltrate this organization. José Antonio Lanuza, spokesperson for the DRE, said that Oswald had offered a $10,000 contribution and his help in military training for an invasion." The *New York Times* also referred to this fact, citing as sources Cuban refugees in New Orleans and Miami. The newspaper noted that during July, Oswald made attempts to join the DRE, in order to participate in the plans to bring down the revolutionary government of Fidel Castro. The representative of the organization, Carlos Bringuier, said that at first he was suspicious of Oswald and that he thought he might be an FBI or a CIA agent trying to find out what the group was doing. Fidel Castro commented: "A pro-Castro American wanting to infiltrate an anti-Castro organization? And without any links to us? Why? If he were a Cuban who wanted to infiltrate . . . It's strange, because they are superinfiltrated with Americans, with FBI and CIA agents inside the organizations. . . "[45]

The DRE episode began on August 5, 1963, when Oswald went to meet with Bringuier, the DRE leader, in New Orleans. Oswald was unemployed and offered to train anti-Castro Cubans; Bringuier promised to pay for the service. Four days later, on August 9, a Cuban friend told Bringuier that three blocks away from his office there was a North American distributing pro-Cuba propaganda. Bringuier went running out to protest and saw it was Oswald who was distributing the pamphlets. They argued, a fight broke out, and the two were arrested for breaching public order.[46] The incident made the news and Oswald appeared in a televised debate with Bringuier, during the course of which he declared that he was a Marxist-Leninist. On August 16 he appeared on television again, distributing pro-Cuba literature in a New Orleans market. Nine days later he participated in another debate with Bringuier, on radio station WDSU, set up by announcer William Stuckey, and with Manuel Gil, head of public relations for the Cuban Revolutionary Council, serving as moderator. He again declared that he was a Marxist. Bringuier's group, already suspicious of Oswald, was now convinced that he had intended to infiltrate the organization. One of Bringuier's aides was sent to penetrate Oswald's "communist cell," but returned with the impression that the "Fair Play for Cuba Committee" didn't exist. Moreover, Oswald had already completed his role: to call public attention to his supposed links with Fidel Castro. He took some money from the DRE and disappeared from

---

[45] *Revolución*. Havana. November 24, 1963.
[46] At the station Oswald asked to see John Quigley, a Dallas FBI agent, who burned all the notes he took during the meeting.

sight for a while. Between August 25 and September 17 there was almost no news of Oswald, except that he was seen by six persons at a registration site for Black voters during a federal electoral campaign in Clinton, Louisiana, approximately 30 miles from New Orleans. He was with David Ferrie and Clay Shaw.

On September 23 Marina Oswald, now pregnant, and her daughter left New Orleans in the company of Ruth Paine, who set them up in a house in Irving, a suburb of Dallas. Paine had known the Oswalds since February, when they lived in that city. On September 25, Oswald took a bus from New Orleans and arrived in Dallas, the first stop on a long journey — destination: Mexico. That night the Cuban sisters Silvia and Annie Odio, who lived in Dallas, received a visit. Their doorbell rang. Annie answered the door; it was three men she didn't know. One of them asked for Silvia. She said that Silvia was getting ready for a party, but they insisted on seeing her and waited in the hall. Annie went to call her and minutes later Silvia appeared. According to Silvia Odio's declarations to the Warren Commission, revealed to the Senate Committee in 1975, two of them were evidently Latinos, and the other a North American who spoke no Spanish. The documents say that Silvia didn't dare affirm that the Latinos were in fact Cubans, but she did state that they seemed to be or could have been Cubans, which seems strange since she herself was Cuban and should have been able to easily identify her fellow countrymen. The taller one said that he was called "Leopoldo," and that the other one was "Angelo," emphasizing that these were noms de guerre — a common custom in anti-Castro circles — and the North American was introduced as "Leon Oswald." The conversation lasted more than 20 minutes. They were close together and the hall was well lit. What called Silvia's attention was the excuse they gave for the visit: that the sisters write a letter soliciting donations from some business people in order to help the "Cuban revolution." She declined, and they argued. They told her that they had come from New Orleans and that they were affiliated with the Junta Revolucionario en Exilio (JURE) [Revolutionary Government in Exile], and referred to her father in prison in Cuba.

The Latinos seemed to be well-informed about Silvia's relations. She and her sister raised money for the JURE, an anti-Castro group, which sprung from Manuel Ray Rivero's MRP, the organization with social democratic leanings that carried out Operation Liborio. In addition to the information provided in Chapter 2, the parents of the sisters, Amador and Sara, were rich landowners in the 1950s and now members of the MRP. They had been in prison in Cuba since October 1961 for having hidden one of the chiefs of Operation Liborio. Silvia's desire to help get her parents out of jail led her and her sisters to maintain relations with politically active Cuban exiles and to join JURE. A few days after the visit, "Leopoldo" telephoned Silvia and told her: "Listen, the American is crazy. . . . Leon Oswald is an ex-Marine, a crack shot, and he says he's going to kill Kennedy. . . . We Cubans have lost face because Kennedy should have been assassinated after the Bay of Pigs. . ."

Silvia also had a good friend named Lucille Connell, who worked for a charity, but she didn't know that Connell was an FBI informant. Watching television the day Kennedy was killed, Silvia recognized Oswald and her other sister Sarita commented almost immediately to Lucille Connell: "It's the guy that was in our house, my sister saw him." Connell informed the FBI: "Listen, the woman says she knows the assassin."

In 1964, Silvia Odio spontaneously decided to tell the Warren Commission about the encounter she had with "Leopoldo" and "Leon Oswald," but they discounted her testimony, saying that she "suffered from nerves." Let us consider that allegation, in light of Silvia's background. In 1960 she was married to a North American in Cuba, and they decided to move to Puerto Rico. They had children, and when they arrived "with nothing but the clothes on their backs" it wasn't easy to build a new life. In 1961 she learned of the imprisonment of her parents in Cuba. In March 1963 she separated from her husband, and with the help of a charity (the one where her FBI informant friend worked) she went with her children to live in Dallas, where she began to find a little tranquility. But since she was already a traumatized person, she suffered a nervous breakdown and was admitted to a psychiatric hospital for a time. A doctor who attended her during her treatment stated that she was in perfect health when she recognized Oswald on television as the North American who had been in the hallway of her apartment.

Silvia's was a key testimony. She knew beforehand from "Leopoldo" that Oswald said that he had to kill Kennedy, and if the Warren Commission accepted her statement it would prove that Oswald formed part of a conspiracy (not exactly pro-Castro). Another of the Warren Commission's arguments was that Silvia could not see well that night (in spite of the facts that the hall was well lit and that she had no vision problems), because Oswald was in Mexico that day, trying to get to Cuba. Nevertheless, the Senate Commission in 1975 recognized that she was telling the truth.

Oswald arrived in Mexico two days later, on September 27. For a long time this fact was only known by his wife Marina, CIA officials in the United States, and a select group at the CIA post in Mexico City. During his bus trip he told two Australians and an English businessman that he intended to go to Cuba from Mexico and meet Castro in person.

In the Mexican capital he stayed at the Hotel Comercio (a refuge for anti-Castro Cubans) and went directly to the Cuban Embassy to request a transit visa that would permit him to spend a few days in Cuba on his way to the Soviet Union. Trying to be friendly with the consular official who attended him, the Mexican Silvia Durán, he showed her newspaper clippings of his dispute with Bringuier, a United States passport that attested to his stay in the Soviet Union, documents naming him as secretary of the FPCC in New Orleans, as well as Communist Party USA credentials. He filled out and signed a form to which he attached a photograph. Cuban diplomats asked for time to respond. From there Oswald went to the Soviet Embassy where he was attended by the official Pavel ("Pablo") Iastkov, to whom he told his story. The official informed him of the difficulties of processing a visa so rapidly, since they were issued in Moscow. Shortly afterwards Silvia Durán telephoned the Soviet Embassy to consult them about Oswald's visa. She talked to "Pablo," who thought that Oswald's case seemed strange, and then reiterated the difficulties of obtaining the visa. The Cubans were inclined to issue Oswald a visa if the Soviets gave him one, but when Oswald returned to the Cuban Embassy, Silvia Durán told him that it was impossible, that the procedure would take at least four months, and that first he had to obtain the Soviet visa. Oswald got angry. He claimed that since he was a friend of Cuba, his visa should be immediately approved. A heated discussion ensued and Cuban consul Eusebio Azcue appeared. To an uncomprehending Oswald, he explained that a person who behaved in such a manner could harm, not help, the Cuban revolution, and he asked him to leave the premises immediately, without the visa. Oswald was so anxious for that document, or for some unknown reason, that it seemed he needed to call attention to himself. At any rate, the bureaucracy impeded such a speedy granting of a visa.

Something very curious happened with the episode in Mexico. Many versions circulated that it was not Oswald at all, but a double, a mysterious impostor. The CIA produced an internal memorandum for the Warren Commission where it alleged that informants in Mexico obtained information and took photos of a man whom they identified as Lee Harvey Oswald who visited the Cuban Embassy on September 27, and who was in Mexico from September 26 to October 3, making several visits to both the Cuban and the Soviet Embassies, trying to get a transit visa to Cuba on his way to Russia. But when the Warren Commission asked the CIA for the photos they took of Oswald in Mexico City, the photos which were produced were of a man who was clearly not Oswald.

Notified of the discrepancy, the CIA simply said that it had made an error: that it had not taken any photos and had no information on the daily movements of Oswald in Mexico, and it had no proof of either the date of his exit or his means of transportation. It also declared that it had a camera pointed in the direction of the Cuban Embassy and had photographed the man who appeared as "the other." A note from FBI Director J. Edgar Hoover, dated November 23, 1963 (one day after the crime in Dallas), supplies other details: "The CIA notified us that on October 1, a very sensitive source [which in the language of espionage means a tape recording] reported on an individual identified as Lee Oswald making contact with the Soviet Embassy in Mexico. Special agents from this bureau who interrogated Oswald in Dallas looked at photographs of the individual referred to earlier and listened to recordings of his voice. These special agents are of the opinion that the individual in question was not Lee Harvey Oswald." Did the officials of this bureau know that according to Jim Garrison's investigations, Lee Harvey Oswald was FBI Agent No. 179? In reference to this affair, the Cuban State Security Department confirmed that the CIA had installed itself in a house facing their embassy and that the Cubans themselves had photographed a CIA agent pointing a camera at the diplomatic building; that microphones were installed in the Cuban chancellery and that the conversations with Oswald were recorded as well as the telephone calls between the Cuban and Soviet Embassies. So what did the Warren Commission do? It suggested that Oswald spent his days in Mexico alone, that he went to the movies, perhaps to the bullfights, and ate at a cheap restaurant near his hotel, but they did not try to find out the motives for his trip.

The indications of CIA meddling in the case intensified when the declarations of both the Mexican writer Elena Garro de Paz, at the time the wife of the famous writer Octavio Paz, and UNAM (National Autonomous University of Mexico) law student Oscar Contreras were made known. The student said he remembered a person from the United States named Harvey Oswald who asked him for help getting a Cuban visa when they met in the UNAM cafeteria. The CIA said that they could not locate Contreras in 1976, the date they decided to do so, but journalist Anthony Summers interviewed Contreras who alleged that the Oswald he saw in Mexico was not the same man who appeared in the newspapers in November as Kennedy's assassin. More important is the account attributed to Elena Garro de Paz, which was relayed in 1965 to Charles William Thomas, an official at the U.S. Embassy in Mexico and a U.S. intelligence agent. It referred to a party on the last night of September 1963, where there were "nothing but communists" and a "strange person dressed in black, a gringo who never took his eyes off the floor," and who Elena Garro later recognized from the newspapers as Lee Harvey Oswald.

This account forms part of the series of documents on the Kennedy assassination, "classified" as confidential, grade III, subject to declassification after 36 years. In 1978, under pressure from Congressmen, seven of these documents were declassified for an investigation by the U.S. House of Representatives, with a justification from the State Department contained in an accompanying letter, explaining that some complete paragraphs had been erased because they could "damage relations between the United States and Latin America or reveal confidential sources or methods that make up part of the operation of our embassy in Mexico." Fragments of the Elena Garro-Oswald case were revealed; the CIA and the FBI were accused of "negligence" by House investigators; Elena Garro declined to make a statement; on the basis of the report by Charles W. Thomas, the conclusion was reached that "the woman was an extremist, a professional anti-Communist, and she would have liked for Castro to have been responsible for the assassination of Kennedy." In their final report they declared that, "The investigation of this committee in Mexico was made impossible by the CIA, who refused to place at our disposal sources relevant to the Elena Garro incident." In spite of the repercussions that they might have, the allegations of the Mexican writer were never explored.[47]

Presented with this picture, they ended up reproducing the puzzle of the "mysterious man in Mexico City" and a series of investigations directed at deciphering it, a fiction plot, leading down a blind alley for more than three decades. Did the real Oswald go to Mexico or not? Oswald's companions on the bus trip to Mexico recognized him later as Kennedy's alleged assassin; handwriting analysis demonstrated that his signature in the register of the Hotel Comercio was authentic; and, more importantly, the visa application was filled out and signed in the Cuban Embassy by Oswald himself, and contains his photo. This document was made available to the Congressional Commission of 1978, which

---

[47] On March 23, 1992, Mexican journalist Gerardo Ochoa Sandy interviewed Elena Garro for the magazine *Proceso*. Garro declared that she did not go to that party and never met Oswald.

confirmed its veracity. Deciphering the mystery of Oswald in Mexico was key to revealing the truth about the assassination of Kennedy. Since Oswald could not obtain the all-important Cuban visa, the wheels of disinformation were set into motion for the purpose of avoiding the arousal of suspicions regarding his relationship to the CIA. Even considering that there could have been another Oswald, the fact is that either the real Oswald was there or that both Oswalds were in Mexico.

Now, who was the CIA official in charge of passing on information about Oswald in Mexico? It was one of the most important figures in the CIA's operations against Fidel Castro: David Atlee Phillips, the master of disinformation, the former chief of propaganda and communications in the Bay of Pigs operation, a man closely linked to figures high up in the military-industrial complex. And what was David Phillips doing in Mexico monitoring the steps of Oswald or the supposed Oswald? In 1963, David Phillips was head of the CIA operations in Mexico. The 1978 Committee was also interested in knowing why the central offices of the Agency were not immediately notified when the Mexican branch discovered that Oswald was thinking of going to Cuba and the Soviet Union. Phillips responded to the inquiry by appealing to the principles of covert operations: "When I became head of Cuban operations and later of Latin American affairs, someone talked to me about this case, or I read about it in the files in the safe. The problem is that the CIA officials involved never commented on their participation in any case, not even with senior officials, except with those who were in the chain of command of the specific plan at the time. And top secret documents are not kept in the office of a department head."[48] The Committee came to an agreement with the Agency in which it was established that any information obtained from the files had to first pass through an examination before being published. David Phillips would not even be mentioned in the final report.

The Dallas-Mexico episode also linked Lee Harvey Oswald with Antonio Veciana, head of Alpha 66. The investigator Gaetón

---

[48] Phillips, David A. *The night watch*. New York. Athenium, 1977.

Fonzi[49] suspected that the man (Leopoldo) who had been with Silvia Odio was actually Veciana, given the references to the MRP. Both JURE and Alpha 66 were cut from the same tree, the only difference was in their methods of struggle. Fonzi also pursued to no avail the idea that David Phillips might be "Maurice Bishop," (the name by which the individual who directed Antonio Veciana's steps was introduced). At the end of September 1963, precisely the date of the Odio incident, Veciana had a meeting with "Bishop" in the lobby of a downtown Dallas building. Arriving at the assigned spot, he saw "Bishop" conversing with a man whom he later recognized as Oswald.

November 22 (UPI) — "Oswald was captured during an exchange of gunfire where he was hiding in a movie theater. . . . Police said that Oswald worked in the Texas School Book Depository. . ." After his frustrated pilgrimage in search of a visa, Oswald returned to Dallas on October 4. The following day he went to Jack Ruby's night club; he needed money. Ruby said that he had to wait until the "job" was finished. Oswald rented a room in Dallas under the pseudonym of O.H. Lee. He got a job in the Texas School Book Depository through Ruth Paine, who had taken care of Marina Oswald. Ruth and her husband Michael Paine were "classified": they were agents of the CIA. When he was detained Oswald told the press: "They arrested me because I lived in the USSR. . . . I am a patsy." Interrogated, Marina said that Oswald was psychotic and violent. Oswald was assassinated by Jack Ruby in front of 70 policemen and the television cameras. There would never be a trial.

On November 23, one day after the death of the President, an official declaration was published by the State Department: "Department authorities said today that there was no evidence to indicate that the USSR or any other power is implicated in the assassination." Prime Minister Fidel Castro's response was, "Why did the State Department have to make this statement? It was revealing for the first time to the other authorities and to the North American public the danger of the anti-Soviet and anti-Cuban

[49] Fonzi, Gaetón. Op cit.

John F. Kennedy

Fidel Castro

Oswald's arrest at the Texas Theater, November 22, 1963

Lee Harvey Oswald at Dallas police headquarters

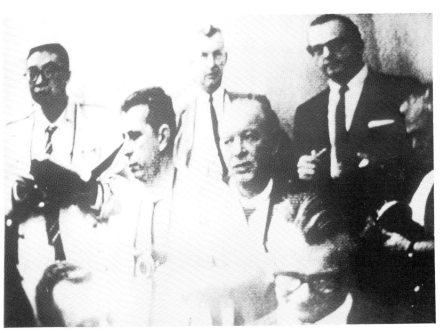

Jack Ruby (top right) at press conference at Dallas police headquarters at midnight November 22, 1963. During the press conference Ruby interjected, naming the Fair Play for Cuba Committee in order to correct a journalist's question about the "pro-Cuba" organization established by Oswald

Jack Ruby (below right) about to shoot Lee Harvey Oswald

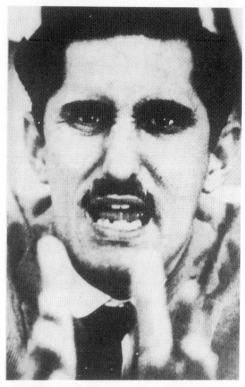

Antonio Veciana

Tony Varona

Sam Giancana

John Roselli

Santos Trafficante

David Atlee Phillips

Howard Hunt

General Maxwell Taylor

Richard Helms

Frank Sturgis

General Edward Lansdale

Photo: Liborio Noval

General Fabián Escalante

campaign that was developing in the most reactionary and bellicose circles of the United States."[50] The State Department itself understood the danger.

Lee Harvey Oswald, Kennedy's "assassin." An enigma? No, a "useful" innocent who left a trail. Oswald in the air base in Japan, in Russia, with the Fair Play for Cuba Committee, with the DRE, with the Blacks of the South, with Silvia Odio, in the Cuban Embassy in Mexico. The "Cubanization" of Oswald was a "way out": it assumed an alignment with the Cuban revolution, but, in fact, his contacts were mainly with anti-Castro groups. Meanwhile, the earlier incidents indicate that Oswald was not associated directly with the anti-Castro groups, but rather with the intelligence community. The final report of the 1978 Congressional Commission distorted all this: "It is possible . . . that Oswald had not thought about assassinating the President at the time of the Odio incident, or on the contrary that the assassination was not related to his anti-Castro contacts and that he was related to them for other reasons." It also concluded that Oswald had no links to the CIA.

Paradoxes are the main characteristic of intelligence operations. Nevertheless, let us apply the principles of mathematics: if the truth is equal to a lie, information belongs to counter-information; if shortcuts intercept the path, denial is plausible; the government, invisible, that multiplied becomes a great entanglement and later a "covert operation." By their very nature they leave no trail, only echoes and dissonant sounds.

---

[50] *Revolución*. Havana. November 24, 1963.

CHAPTER 5

Uniting the points

Dissent within the Kennedy government
A hero of the Second World War, 44 years old, charismatic, capable, a millionaire, a brilliant career as a Democratic senator, the descendant of Irish aristocrats and a Catholic (there had never before been a Catholic president), John Fitzgerald Kennedy defeated Richard Nixon, the vice-president of the out-going Republican administration in the U.S. presidential elections of November 1960, by a margin of a hundred thousand votes.

The Kennedy government brought a new political style into the center of the Cold War structures implanted under the aegis of presidents Truman and Eisenhower, introducing the vision of the "businessman" in contrast to the politics of the hardliners. Nevertheless, he would pay dearly for these reforms. In the almost three years of his administration, various points of internal tension developed, the most outstanding being the measures to broaden civil rights and the ending of racial segregation in the South; disagreements with the great "trusts" on labor questions; the creation of the Alliance for Progress; difficulties with the interests of the military-industrial complex; the persecution of organized crime; and conflicts with the CIA and anti-Castro Cuban exile groups. In the succession of events, Kennedy acted to neutralize or alleviate the areas of tension, avoiding a direct confrontation; and viewed in a linear or simplistic fashion, the President's theory or the practice could appear ambiguous. At the same time, Kennedy would also change his position when faced with new circumstances, revealing his commitment to reform.

However, all of the skill that he displayed did not prevent the power bloc from escaping his control. One individual could not direct either the system or the process; the 1960s heralded a world in upheaval. Throughout his term in office the divergent tendencies increased, making coexistence impossible between the reformer, the establishment and the other circles of power that continued to act according to their own principles and interests. There were also other problems common to all state bureaucracies. Dean Rusk, Kennedy's Secretary of State, gave orders to the ambassadors, but they took other positions, being appointees of the Eisenhower administration. The ideal U.S. Democrat suffered his setbacks.

One of the most significant examples of the period was the conflict between Kennedy and the military-industrial complex, whose influence was felt in many sectors of U.S. society. At the beginning of his government, Kennedy had to confront the problem of Vietnam. To maintain a permanent division of that country (north and south) and impede its reunification — as Ho Chi Minh's forces (in the north) and the Viet Cong (in the south) desired — President Eisenhower had decided to use military advisers under the control of the CIA. The U.S. military-industrial complex was already prepared to act firmly in the region; nevertheless, according to General Maxwell Taylor, Kennedy refused to use large-scale military forces as some Pentagon officials wished. He did, however, agree to modestly increase the number of military advisers. Then the problem of Laos arose. General Maxwell Taylor and McNamara were under pressure from the military, but the President did not want to run the risk of losing the war. He tried to apply a different foreign policy, although still confronting communism and the socialist bloc: the theory of "low intensity warfare," that is, wherever there was a revolutionary war, send in advisers.

In June 1961, Kennedy held talks with Khrushchev, taking the first steps against the arms race and atmospheric nuclear testing. Two months later a wall was erected in Berlin which Khrushchev regarded as a defensive measure. Kennedy avoided discussing the topic in public so as not to spark speculation that he was accepting the division of the world, but he did nothing to stop it. In October there was a confrontation between Soviet and U.S. tanks in Berlin, which ended with a secret message from Kennedy to Khrushchev that the tanks must be withdrawn "without damaging the prestige of either side."[51]

In July 1962, in the face of increasing demands of U.S. and world public opinion, Kennedy resolved to withdraw from Vietnam. He instructed Robert McNamara, the Secretary of Defense, to begin a plan to pull out the advisers (which was to be concluded by the end of 1965). In May 1963, he revealed confidentially to certain anti-war senators that he planned to completely withdraw the U.S. forces if he were re-elected, although he publicly denied such an intention. He told Senator Mansfield that he could not do this prior to the 1964 elections, because in the campaign the Republicans would use the argument that the Democrats had lost in Indochina. In June, at the American University in Washington, Kennedy spoke out in favor of peace. "If we cannot end our differences now, we can at least contribute to making the world safe in its diversity. . . . We must change our attitudes toward the USSR" and put an end to "the vicious circle where the suspicions of one side generate suspicions in the other." He warned that "the production of new weapons transforms the nation into an armed country." In July, Kennedy drew up a new agreement with Khrushchev to ban nuclear explosions in the atmosphere. In October 1963, he signed NSAM 263 (a National Security Council act), ordering the withdrawal of one thousand of the 16,000 military advisers stationed in Vietnam. These measures did not meet with the approval of the ultra right wing in the United States who supported an open confrontation with the Soviet Union and a greater use of U.S. military force in solving problems in foreign countries.

In the midst of this panorama, the Alliance for Progress appeared. Seen by some as a political step forward, by some as a

---

[51] Bechloss, Michael. *The crisis years: Kennedy and Khrushchev 1960-1963.* New York. Harper Collins Publishers, Inc. 1990.

step backward, and by others as a palliative that would not get to the root of Latin America's problems, the Alliance for Progress represented a new tactic in foreign policy and a different view of Latin American problems. It signified that the United States was resolved to take the lead in the process of reform and neutralize the influence of the Cuban revolution in Latin America by identifying itself with progressive forces and proposing an "orderly" revolution which would be compatible with its interests. On the other hand, by freeing itself from the Pentagon's path of war and confrontation with the oligarchies, it gave more breathing space to the Cuban revolution.

Furthermore, after the Alliance for Progress was initiated, there was a growing tendency for military regimes to emerge in Latin America. Elected or constitutional governments were overthrown or impeded from taking power by the military, even though Kennedy demonstrated his disapproval. After the coups in Honduras and Peru in 1962, his administration suspended aid programs to those countries and refused to recognize the new governments until the military promised to hold free elections and respect civil liberties. According to Robert Kennedy, this policy was criticized by politicians who would later be integrated into the State Department during Lyndon Johnson's administration.

On organized crime, John Kennedy, when he was still a senator, participated in several commissions dealing with illegal activities of the Mafia. As president, one of the priorities of his Attorney General, Robert Kennedy, was to combat the activities of the big Mafia capos. At the same time, by developing a policy opposed to the racism in the southern states, he made enemies of the segregationists, Democrats and Republicans alike. The first Black student to enroll in a southern university did so because of a presidential order and under the protection of the National Guard.

As has already been amply demonstrated, the Kennedy's attitude to the Cuban government was reflected in various incidents which, from our point of view, represent the crux of the problem. President Fidel Castro, analyzing Kennedy's stand during the Bay of Pigs invasion, observed in a 1992 tripartite meeting on the Missile Crisis: "I don't blame Kennedy for the Bay of Pigs invasion.

He didn't like the operation, and he had the authority to stop it; but sometimes during a first term a leader doesn't always handle policies well. He labored very calmly at the beginning of the incident that was heading toward a military disaster, he demonstrated prudence and valor by assuming responsibility for the acts." When he learned the grotesque details of Operation Pluto, Kennedy tried to keep the prestige of the United States from being further damaged. Richard Nixon, in his memoirs, related a conversation that he had with the President the day after the Bay of Pigs disaster. Kennedy apparently said, "I was persuaded by all those sons of bitches — all the military specialists and the CIA — who assured me that the plan would succeed. . . . What would you do about Cuba now?" Nixon responded, "I would find an appropriate legal cover and continue. . . . There are many justifications that can be used, such as protecting U.S. citizens residing in Cuba and the defense of our base in Guantánamo." Kennedy shook his head, reflecting, "If the United States were to take Cuba, Khrushchev could take Berlin." This wasn't just a casual observation: Kennedy began to reflect on Cuba in a global political context, which indicated a need for caution. As a consequence of his decision, Kennedy would find himself obliged to contend with the disgust of the anti-Castro groups, which would never forgive him for not having given the order for an aerial bombardment. The exiles wanted more than the intermittent attention that the President conceded to them after the disaster of the Bay of Pigs. They wanted his unquestionable support for the liquidation of the regime in power in Cuba.

Within the CIA itself, which Kennedy blamed for the blunder, there was disagreement. The Inspector General, Lymon Kirkpatrick, made a report that was never declassified, directly accusing CIA director Allen Dulles and the other directors of "black operations," of having conspired behind the backs of the CIA and the entire intelligence system. Kirkpatrick concluded that the operation was doomed from the beginning, because everyone knew that its success depended upon internal support within Cuba, and the only resistance to Castro came from Miami. This denunciation clashed with the norms of protection of covert operations. Dulles called Kirkpatrick and asked him to rewrite the text in a different tone. In reality, Kirkpatrick's only error was not recognizing that the operations were not outside the structure of the Agency, but rather one of its principal foundations. A month later, aware that Kennedy disapproved of its methods, the CIA decided to develop Operation Patty, the plan to attack the Guantánamo Naval Base and assassinate the Castro brothers. At that time General Taylor was preparing his report and the Agency had supposedly frozen its work, waiting for new guidelines.

On the basis of the Taylor Report, the President signed a series of National Security Memorandums, two of which are worth mentioning here: No. 55 instructed the Joint Chiefs of Staff to evaluate the resources available to U.S. military and paramilitary forces, examining their state of readiness and preparation for the Cold War. Memorandum No. 57 demanded that the clandestine operations of the CIA be secret and deniable, noting that the Bay of Pigs invasion did not obey these principles. It also decreed that future operations of the Agency which required military logistical support must be carried out under the direction of the Pentagon. General Charles Cabell, deputy director of the CIA, was instructed that his own chief of staff should be in charge of paramilitary actions.

At the same time that memorandum 55 discouraged the arms race, taking into consideration only the readiness of the armed forces for any eventuality, No. 57 subordinated the CIA to the Pentagon in the area of military actions. The President was attacking on the two fronts, trying to maintain them under his control, since he needed both for his counterinsurgency plans throughout the world. The man he selected to supervise the actions of the CIA was his brother Robert Kennedy, busy at the time with the question of civil rights and the fight against the Mafia.

While he began this attack, another plot to assassinate Castro was being carried out by the CIA. This was Operation Liborio. Although some of the investigators knew about the plots, neither Patty nor Liborio was mentioned by the Senate Intelligence Committee in 1975, because the CIA had covered both of them up. Richard Bissell, who at the time of these plans was the head of covert operations, told the senators of the committee that he believed that Allen Dulles had in some way informed Kennedy about these operations.

With the birth of Mongoose, a strategy accepted by all of the U.S. governmental apparatus, there was a restructuring of the cadres of the Agency. President Kennedy removed Allen Dulles and Richard Bissell, and designated John McCone and Richard Helms to fill their respective posts. In this new situation the CIA began to form its invisible government, the operative structure that would take charge of the Cuban case: Task Force W and the huge base in Florida, the JM Wave.

Having facilitated the CIA's carrying out of covert actions, Kennedy would end up confronting a force of uncontrollable dimensions. Although the general outline of the Mongoose plan, which contained a timetable for the invasion of Cuba in 1962, was known to President Kennedy, this did not mean that all of its programs — through military or secret channels — were. The top directors of the Agency do not occupy political posts in the strictest sense of the word; they are professionals who design and carry out plans financed by third parties; they work in the underground and end up being those who make the real decisions. Not only did the President not know all the details of the operations, but practically no one else did either, since the CIA never reports everything. There are also doubts about the extent to which Robert Kennedy, appointed to supervise the Agency, was informed. When Robert McNamara was asked about this in Havana in 1992, he alleged that he knew nothing. John McCone, placed at the head of the CIA by Kennedy in order to help control it, was never able to penetrate the real workings of the Agency.

An example of this was the reaction of the covert apparatus of the Agency to recommendations of the Special Amplified Group (SAG), the executive board of Mongoose. When it was established that all explicit details of the large intelligence operations should be submitted for approval before being put into action, Richard Helms decided to act on his own. He gave explicit orders to William Harvey, head of Task Force W and ZR Rifle, to reactivate the poison capsule project without the need for any other approval.

Helms admitted to the 1975 Senate Committee that he had not been instructed by anyone to proceed with the capsule plot, and that he had not even informed his director, John McCone, one of the members of the SAG. Nobody knows for certain how Richard Helms and William Harvey communicated. What is known is that, at the end of April 1962, when the capsules were again sent to Cuba, General Lansdale knew about it.

As October 1962 approached, there was a public relations campaign, which included resolutions in Congress, intended to pressure the Kennedy administration into a war. But the unfolding of the Missile Crisis disenchanted the most ardent hawks. Kennedy had blocked the finale of the already inept Operation Mongoose: military intervention. The response of the U.S. President to the discovery of the missiles by Military Intelligence and the CIA was a blow to them. Kennedy and his group were resolved to use diplomacy rather than force. He would negotiate the crisis, taking advantage of Khrushchev's weakness, and achieve his objectives. Fidel Castro later observed: "With respect to Khrushchev and Kennedy, I regard the first with friendship and respect. The second, independent of the conflicts that arose in the era, I consider to be a valiant man who consolidated his leadership after the crisis, and the President in the best position to rectify some of the aspects of U.S. policy toward Cuba."[52] In fact, Kennedy emerged stronger from the crisis. He emerged as an able statesman who did not adopt a hawkish position and who was seen to be unjust toward Cuba only because his instructions on Cuba were ignored. The agreements with Khrushchev provoked claims that Kennedy was a communist sympathizer. According to U.S. researcher Michael Bechloss, at that time George Bush, the head of the Republican Party in Houston, Texas, told Kennedy that he should "gather up the courage to invade Cuba."

In January 1963, General Lansdale wrote a memorandum stating that Operation Mongoose would be "discontinued." During the course of the following months, the CIA would continue its covert

---

[52] Tripartite Conference on the Missile Crisis. Closing speech of President Fidel Castro. Havana, January, 1992.

and terrorist actions designed to liquidate the Cuban revolution.

But, on the part of the Kennedy government, a dual strategy was developed with respect to Cuba: they announced their willingness to open dialogue, hoping to separate Cuba from the Soviet orbit, while at the same time approving 13 "covert actions" — predominantly of an economic nature — against the country. In that way, Kennedy implemented the alternative outlined but not recommended in Mongoose, option A (the "blockade"), which in reality had never been interrupted, but which indicated that it was now admissible to accept the existence of the Cuban government. He was no longer the Kennedy of 1961, forced to play with a marked deck: he had decided to win by other means, more pragmatic and with an acceptable political cost, without an invasion and without a war. More than ever, the Cuban question came to be the central source of conflict between the President and the supporters of a policy of aggression. In Washington two principal and opposing tendencies began to coexist: the Kennedys' policy, in favor of economic asphyxiation, and the other group, which included the CIA, for more direct action against Cuba.

The anti-Castro Cuban exiles and Kennedy had very different opinions of one another. For the President, the group as such was unimportant, although he considered that they had a role to play in the undermining of the influence of Fidel Castro and communist ideas among Latin Americans. Nevertheless, the counter-revolutionaries demanded more and more that he take a clear position against the Cuban revolution. A decisive moment came when a group of terrorists intensified their activities, and the U.S. government intervened. According to Veciana, the leader of Alpha 66, "The purpose was to put Kennedy up against the wall and force him to move against Castro." Resentment spread through the CIA and the counterrevolutionary groups due to the repression of the commandos. By the second quarter of 1963, it was already being said that Kennedy should die because he was a traitor and a communist.

Another important event took place in September and October 1963. At the request of McGeorge Bundy, the adviser to the U.S. delegation at the United Nations (William Attwood) went to find out from Carlos Lechuga (the Cuban Ambassador) what the attitude of the Cuban government would be toward a proposal for normalizing relations between the two countries. The meeting between Attwood and Lechuga took place at the home of Lisa Howard. News of the meeting circulated in U.S. power circles, causing panic. At the time, the Kennedy reelection campaign was in full swing, and some public opinion polls showed his popularity declining. Also, his speech in Florida on November 18, 1963, to a conference of the InterAmerican Press Society disappointed the anti-Castro Cubans and the supporters of a confrontation with Cuba. The press agencies reported: "Miami, Florida — Thousands of exiles attended an open air meeting awaiting Kennedy's arrival. They waited in vain that night for a firm promise from Kennedy that he would take energetic measures against the communist regime of Fidel Castro." They listened as the President said: "We in the hemisphere must utilize all of the resources at our disposal to impede the establishment of another Cuba in this hemisphere," a statement which suggested that the reality of Cuba had been accepted. According to UPI, "Three editors of Latin American dailies criticized today the weak attitude of President Kennedy toward the liquidation of the communist regime of Castro in Cuba. . . . Julio Mesquita Filho, director of the Brazilian daily *El Estado de Sao Paulo*, who moved the editors of the InterAmerican Press Society yesterday with an analysis of the economic and political situation of his country, said that the United States has made an error in not comprehending in time the danger that the presence of Cuba signified for the entire continent. Mesquita demonstrated his support for collective and armed action in the hemisphere against Cuba, because he was a defender of the free self-determination of peoples. . . . Sergio Carbó, editor of the *Prensa Libre*, a confiscated Havana daily, and director of the executive board of the IPS, declared that he considered that a grave event in the near future would oblige Washington to change its policy of peaceful coexistence."

A month before the assassination of Kennedy, the French journalist Jean Daniel reported to Ambassador Attwood that he was on his way to Cuba for a meeting with Fidel Castro. Attwood communicated this to McGeorge Bundy (Kennedy's National Security Adviser) and the U.S. President decided to talk to the journalist before he went to Havana. At this meeting Kennedy affirmed that the menace of Soviet influence in the hemisphere — and not the domestic policies of Castro — was the only reason which justified efforts to isolate and destabilize Cuba. These and other statements were published in *The New Republic* magazine on December 14, 1963. The President added, "We know perfectly well what happened in Cuba, for the misfortune of all. At the beginning I watched the development of these facts with much concern, but my conclusions go beyond those of European analysts. I believe that there is no other country, including those in Africa and others under colonial domination, where there has been more humiliation and exploitation than in Cuba, in part attributable to the policies of my country during the Batista regime. I believe that we contributed to creating and building the Cuban movement, in spite of the form that it took. The accumulation of these errors has put all of Latin America in danger. The cry of the Alliance for Progress was to reverse this erroneous policy. This is one of the greatest, if not the greatest, problem of American foreign policy. I can assure you that I understand the Cubans. I approved of the proclamation that Fidel Castro made in the Sierra Maestra when he called for justice and the liberation of Cuba from corruption." After a pause the President continued, "But it is also true that the problem stopped being Cuban alone, and became international; it became a Soviet problem. Castro betrayed the promises made in the Sierra Maestra, becoming a nonaligned country while agreeing to become a Soviet agent in Latin America. . . . His obsession for independence came from nationalism and not from communist doctrine, as President De Gaulle observed. . . . In any case, Latin American nations will neither progress nor attain justice through the path of communist subversion." Daniel's final question concerned the success of the U.S. blockade against Cuba. Kennedy replied: "Two dikes are necessary to contain Soviet expansion: the blockade on one hand, and on the other a tremendous effort in the direction of progress."

On November 19, 1963, the French journalist was in Havana interviewing Prime Minister Fidel Castro for the same magazine.

Informed of Kennedy's comments, Castro observed that the U.S. president was "sincere and a realist in spite of the transgressions and errors for which he was not completely responsible." He added that "Kennedy increasingly understands that it is impossible to simply contain Cuba and force us — as well as the explosive Latin American situation — to disappear. . . . All of the power and the dollars were in the hands of one class, which Kennedy described when he referred to Batista. . . . What's happening now? The [U.S.] trusts see that their interests are being compromised, the Pentagon thinks that its strategic bases are in danger, the powerful oligarchies throughout Latin America alert their friends in the United States, who then sabotage the new policy, and soon Kennedy has the whole world against him. . ."

In his interview with Daniel, Castro spoke at length about the determination of his country to resist a U.S. invasion before the 1962 Missile Crisis: "The United States was the only one that risked using the threat of war to suppress revolutions, not the Cubans or the Soviets. . . . Now I ask only one thing of the United States: leave us in peace." Daniel explained to Castro the basic complaint of Washington: the fact that Cuba was espousing communism and affiliating itself with the Soviet Union. The Cuban leader responded: "Asking me to say that I am not a piece of the Soviet chess game is the same as asking a woman to shout in public that she is not a prostitute." Later he added, "I cannot wait for a leader to come from the United States with a proposal of peace and love. Really, it seems to me that a man like Kennedy is capable of seeing that it is not in the best interests of the United States to maintain a policy that only leads to a stalemate. So we understand that everything can return to normal on the basis of a mutual respect for sovereignty."

Daniel's presence represented the beginning of a dialogue between the two presidents. Castro himself reiterated in January 1992 that President Kennedy had asked the journalist to deliver to him a message of rapprochement. Two days later Kennedy was assassinated in Dallas. Daniel was present when the Cuban leader received the news of the assassination. Castro stood up and said, "Everything has changed. Everything is going to change. . . . [T]he

Cold War, relations with the Soviet Union, with Cuba, the question of the Blacks. . ." And, aware that Vice-President Lyndon Johnson would assume the post, Castro asked, "What authority does he exercise over the CIA?"

CHAPTER 6

The assassination conspiracy

When I arrived in Cuba, I was exhausted by the stratagems of Mr. **X**. He had said that Kennedy was a victim of the CIA and the military who opposed his plans to withdraw from Vietnam and thwart the plots against Fidel Castro. He accused Allen Dulles, whom Kennedy had removed from his post as head of the CIA; General Charles Cabell, brother of the mayor of Dallas and vice director of the CIA; and a mysterious man called General **Y**.

According to newspaper reports,[53] confirmed by the Cuban State Security Department, **X** is a person based on Air Force Colonel Fletcher Prouty, ex-director of special (or dirty) operations of the Pentagon at the beginning of the 1960s — operations which included assassinations, propaganda campaigns and rigging elections in foreign countries. Prouty was the link for Operation Pluto between the Pentagon and the CIA; he later admitted that the Bay of Pigs was a "covert operation." He is now a well-known defender of the conspiracy theory on the Kennedy assassination. General Charles Cabell was removed from the Agency at the same time as Allen Dulles. General Edward Lansdale, the coordinator of

---

[53] *Esquire*, November 1991 and *Time*, December 23, 1991.

Operation Mongoose, was alluded to directly as **Y**. But how true
are Prouty's allegations? How far did the plot extend?

The following is the reasoning of the Cuban State Security
Department. You must distinguish between three levels of
conspiracy, related but distinct: the assassination itself, the
operation to involve Castro in the crime, and the machinations to
undermine the investigations. Let us look at the facts. Kennedy was
assassinated on November 22, 1963, at 12:30 p.m. local time in
Dealey Plaza in the center of Dallas, Texas, while riding in an open
car in an official party, being greeted by the people. As of today,
these are the only elements that have not been questioned by the
international community. All the rest remain as questions,
legitimate or otherwise.

With respect to the third level — the unleashing of the
machinery of disinformation — this is described in the actual
reports of the official commissions and in the private investigations
into Kennedy's death, supported by statements from doctors,
police, representatives of the authorities, and ordinary citizens,
resulting in a large range of contradictions. The following is a brief
summary of these questions.

•*On the origin of the shots* — Abraham Zapruder was standing on
a cement block on Elm Street, filming the presidential car with a
Super 8.[54] In Zapruder's film the President, when he was shot, fell
to the left and was thrown backwards. Considering that point of
view, the shots came from the front and to the right of the
presidential limousine, that is from a position situated behind
Zapruder's camera where there was a wooden fence with a line of
bushes on a grassy knoll, and farther back, a viaduct next to the
railroad tracks. At that exact moment, the Texas School Book
Depository (from which Lee Harvey Oswald is alleged to have
fired) was well behind and to the right of Kennedy. The attention
of most of the people in Dealey Plaza was drawn to the area behind
the fence after the sequence of shots. Some people climbed to the
top of the knoll and across the fence in the direction of the railroad

[54] This film was hidden from the public for five years, locked away by *Time*
magazine.

yard. Three men carrying weapons were detained when they fled toward an empty wagon of a train that was commencing to move, but they were later freed by police authorities. No record was kept of their names or their fingerprints, and no report was made of their activity.[55]

Statements which would have confirmed the hypothesis that the shots came from the fence on the grassy knoll, such as those made by Julia Ann Mercer and Lee Bowers, Jr., were discounted. Mercer noticed a truck parked irregularly at the foot of the knoll, more or less an hour before the arrival of Kennedy's caravan. Interrogated by the FBI, she recognized Jack Ruby in a photograph, as the man who drove the truck and helped another take a rifle out of its case. Bowers, Jr., the railroad guard, saw two men standing behind the fence on the knoll watching the caravan approach, who appeared to have something in their hands. At the moment the shots were fired he saw something like a flash of light in the place where the men had been. Other important statements of the same nature were made by J.C. Price, a construction worker; S.M. Holland, the supervisor of the Union Terminal Company; Seymour Weitzman, assistant to the mayor of Dallas; police on duty in the area; and railroad employees. But the Warren Commission Report concluded that "no credible declaration suggested that the shots were fired from the railroad viaduct on the lower triple pass, from the neighboring rail yard or any other place, other than from the book depository building" and that the man who fired the shots was Oswald. The news media promoted this version, and those who rejected it were branded as irresponsible speculators.

• *The additional testimony obtained by the FBI which was not recorded in the Warren Report* — This included testimony by Arnold and Barbara Rowland, Carolyn Walther, Tony Henderson and Amos Euin. Their testimonies attest to the presence of a "dark skinned man" on the sixth floor of the book depository building

---

[55] The photos of these "vagabonds" were taken by the professional press photographers William Allen (*Dallas Times Herald*), Joe Smith (*Fort Worth Star*) and Jack Bears (*Dallas Morning News*) when they passed the book depository building.

with a rifle in his hands. The Rowlands thought this person was from the U.S. Secret Service. Henderson saw another man, in addition to the "dark skinned man," in the window, and Euin saw a tube projecting out of the window as the presidential caravan entered Elm Street. FBI agents told the witnesses to forget what they had seen. Senator John Powell and others who were watching the parade from the sixth floor of the public jail, facing the book depository, also saw two men in the window with a rifle, one of them Black, and thought that they were security guards. Other people who were behind the presidential caravan heard shots from another building, near the corner of Houston and Elm. Analyzing the set of these observations, New Orleans District Attorney Jim Garrison concluded that a picture of the sixth floor of the book depository before and during the assassination, "would include at least three men, two whites (a young man with dyed blond hair, and a fat man with horn rimmed glasses) and a dark man, of Latino origin."[56]

•*On the number of shots* — Other persons besides Zapruder captured views of the assassination from various angles, including some photographers who were in the center of Dealey Plaza. Analyzing some of these images and sounds, the House Committee on Assassinations affirmed in 1978 that President Kennedy was hit by two bullets from the sixth floor of the book depository, fired by Oswald. Concurring with the Warren Commission, the House Committee concluded that the bullet that hit Texas Governor John Connally (who was sitting in the front seat of the vehicle), was one of those which first hit President Kennedy. Meanwhile, finding evidence of a fourth projectile which hit nothing, shot from the front by a second marksman, the report of the 1978 committee contradicted the Warren Commission pronouncement regarding three shots (two accurate) and a lone gunman: Oswald. Years later, in 1982, the Acoustic Ballistics Commission of the National Investigating Council declared that the 1978 report was not

---

[56] The House Committee on Assassinations concluded that the frontal shot came from the knoll, but missed its target and was fired by another man who "could have been acting independently of Oswald."

scientifically valid. Some documentaries shown at the end of 1988 used the same documents as the House Committee: that of Chris Plumley, for a Catalan radio station, attempted to demonstrate the existence of six shots, based on a tape recording by a Dallas motorist; one for British television featured a Polaroid photo by Mary Ann Moorman which showed a man dressed in a police uniform firing a rifle from the bushes. For lawyer Mark Lane[57] the magic bullet theory — which alleges that the shot from the depository hit Kennedy and then immediately traveled acrobatically through the body of Governor Connally — is unsustainable. Otherwise, you would have to admit that the bullet possessed supernatural powers. At least two projectiles had to have been fired to inflict the wound in Kennedy's throat and all of those suffered by Connally. Another bullet hit the President's head, while another missed the limousine and its occupants, and hit the curb on the southern side of the main street. Therefore, Lane, concluded there were four shots.

•*On Kennedy's wounds* — President Kennedy died in Parkland Hospital at 1:00 p.m. The admission form signed by Dr. Robert McLelland described the cause of death as an "extensive encephalic cerebral lesion caused by a wound in the left temporal provoked by a firearm." Other doctors from Parkland who examined the President — the assistant surgeon Dr. Malcolm Perry and the Chief of Neurosurgery, Dr. Kemp Clark — observed two wounds and stated that the small one in the throat was where the bullet entered, and the large one in the back of the cranium was where it exited. Faced with the Parkland doctors' version, on November 29 the police reconstructed the shooting to prove that the entry wound was the one in the back. *Life* magazine came up with a theory that the President had turned his head completely around at that moment, and for that reason the bullet hit him from behind. U.S. Secret Service agents found the Parkland doctors and told them that the wounds had been inflicted from the side. The declaration that Jacqueline Kennedy made at the time of the shooting was suppressed. The federal police confiscated photographs and x-rays

---

[57] See: Lane, Mark. *Kennedy, the crime and the farce*. 1992.

of the wounds and the tape recordings of the interviews with the Parkland doctors. It is possible that these documents will not be released until the year 2029.

The autopsy of the President was performed in an illegal and incomplete manner. The law specifies that it be done in Texas, but the U.S. Secret Service abducted Kennedy's body and took it by plane to the Naval Hospital in Bethesda, Maryland. The autopsy was directed by an unidentified general who ordered military doctors not to explore the neck, and the three pathologists did not examine the throat wound. One of the doctors received instructions not to discuss the case. The first written version of their findings was incinerated. The photographs and x-rays taken of the body during the autopsy were kept by the U.S. Secret Service. To top it off, the President's brain disappeared. It is evident that there was manipulation of the corpse.

All of the declarations made to the Warren Commission suggested that the bullet came from behind. During District Attorney Jim Garrison's investigations, Dr. John Nichols, a renowned pathologist, analyzed photographs of Zapruder's film and concluded that the fatal shot came from the front, but that he was also hit from behind, from two different positions and at two different angles. These affirmations were also in contradiction with the Warren Commission's theory.

•*On the rifle* — The same day as the assassination, Dallas authorities communicated to the press that the weapon found on the sixth floor of the book depository building was a high precision German Mauser 7.65 rifle. Three empty shells from a Mannlicher Carcano were "found" near the window on the sixth floor, although it is well known that when this weapon is fired, the shells are thrown many meters away.

The FBI confirmed that Lee Harvey Oswald had purchased a Mannlicher Carcano 6.5 by mail order under the pseudonym of "Hiddell." Trying to eliminate the contradiction, the authorities then announced that the rifle found on the sixth floor was not a Mauser, but rather the Carcano. As for fingerprints, normally considered objective proof, the necessary adjustments also were made to these: on the day of the assassination Oswald's prints were not found on the rifle he was said to have used to kill the President, but the following week authorities confirmed that they had been discovered. Oswald submitted to a nitrate test, the results of which demonstrated that he had not fired a rifle in the past 24 hours. A film entrusted to the "Dallas Cinema Association" which showed the assassin's rifle, pictured a weapon without a telescopic sight, which is not consistent with the characteristics of either a Mauser or a Carcano. Nevertheless, those responsible for the investigation proclaimed that, since a fired weapon existed (the old Carcano bought by Oswald under the pseudonym), that was proof of the assassination. There is strong evidence that the photo on the cover of *Life* magazine, which had been provided by Ruth Paine, where Oswald appears carrying a rifle, was a montage.

What in particular contradicts the incrimination of Oswald is the relationship between the quality of the rifle, its origin, and the number of shots fired in the possible time. It has been demonstrated that it was impossible to fire the three shots from the window of the book depository, hit the President with the vision obstructed by a tree and with an old manual rifle (the Mannlicher Carcano) in a space of 5.6 seconds. In the hands of any marksman, at least 2.3 seconds are necessary between each shot. Also, two minutes after the last shot in Dealey Plaza the police found Lee Harvey Oswald in the second floor dining room, calmly drinking a soda. It also seems illogical that Oswald would have done all those things: hid the rifle under a box, gone down four flights of stairs without being out of breath, and purchase a soda — all in such a short space of time. There is one other aspect which is no less important: given the precision of the shots, the perpetrators had to have been excellent, well-trained professionals, serious and patient marksmen, and Oswald was not a good shot.

•*On Oswald's arrest* — At 12:45 (15 minutes after the assassination), the police radio broadcast a bulletin to the patrol cars describing the suspect as "white, thin male, weighing approximately 70 kg, around 1.8 meters tall, and some 30 years old." This was a description which coincided with that of Lee Harvey Oswald.

According to Earlene Roberts, the desk clerk at the guest house where Oswald lived, he was there at approximately 1 p.m., he entered his room (where he took his revolver), he put on a sweater, and went out again. She saw him for the last time waiting for a bus on the same side of the street as the house. A few minutes later, a kilometer away and in the opposite direction from which Oswald was headed, the policeman Tippit was murdered beside his patrol car. The police radio carried a description of the murderer, which also fitted Oswald in general terms. The idea was planted of a single suspect for those two crimes among the thousands of Dallas residents.

Only two of the 13 witnesses testifying to the policeman's murder could reconstruct it: Helen Markham and Domingo Benavides. Markham did not describe any physical characteristics of the assassin when the police arrived at the scene. At the police station, she was shown a lineup which included Oswald. At first she didn't recognize any of them as the man who had killed the policeman. According to Mark Lane, the Dallas prosecutor made five attempts. Since he needed a quick identification, he pressed for a positive response on Oswald, contrary to the norms of the penal process. Markham, nervous, under pressure, and hesitant, agreed to the identification. Domingo Benavides, whose declaration was taken by a Warren Commission lawyer, did not identify Oswald. Helen Markham's was the only testimony upon which the Warren Commission could accuse Oswald of the death of Tippit. But days before testifying before the Commission, she told Mark Lane that the killer of the policeman was short and fat.

The statements of Earlene Roberts were also considered by the Warren Commission, in spite of the difference in the direction she said Oswald was headed to wait for the bus, the possibility of arriving where Tippit was in time to murder him, and the color of the sweater Oswald was wearing when he left the house (a dark color) which did not coincide with that of the (light colored) sweater found at the the scene of the crime. Of the four bullets extracted from Tippit's body, three were Winchester-Western brand, and one was Remington-Peters. Of the four shells found at the scene of the crime, two were Winchester, and two Remington. Important eye witnesses (A. Clemons and a couple named Wright) were discounted: they said that they had seen two men standing beside Tippit's car at the time of the shooting, lending credence to the conclusion that there were two weapons.

One witness said that the man used a 32 caliber automatic pistol; and a policeman reported that the suspect was armed with a 38 automatic. Both differed from the weapon found on Oswald, a 38 revolver. Nevertheless, the Warren Commission arrived at the conclusion that there were credible reasons to believe that Oswald not only killed the President, but also the policeman. This would also be confirmed by the House Committee in 1978.

There is, however, no question about the fact that Oswald went to the Texas Theater, a movie house in Oak Cliff. He was seen walking down the street and entering the movie house without paying by Johnny Brewer, a manager of the store next door. At that moment the radio was broadcasting information on the suspect in the shootings of Tippit and Kennedy, giving a description for both that could fit Oswald. Brewer went to the door of the theater and notified the ticket seller. The police were called. Within a few minutes several police officers arrived, accompanied by FBI agents. They went inside the theater and arrested Oswald, who was carrying a 38 revolver. The Dallas police arrested Oswald for Tippet's murder and only at 1:30 p.m. the following day was he accused of assassinating Kennedy.

The police authorities ended up having to explain why Oswald was sought in such a precipitated manner. Lt. Curry said that it was because of the rifle found at the depository (the Mauser or the Carcano?). The Dallas DA explained that the police who entered the school book depository along with the manager of the building suspected Oswald because he was not at his post (48 employees were not at their posts at that moment and many were forbidden from entering). The Warren Commission admitted that it did not know the answer to this question, but that the arrest had been made as a consequence of the description transmitted by the police radio at 12:45 on November 22, based "primarily" upon the observation of one Howard Brennan, who saw a person in the sixth floor window of the book depository, from the opposite sidewalk, without even noticing the shirt he was wearing.

As the years passed, new twists appeared. As long as it remained a subject of discussion, the mystery remained of whether or not there was a conspiracy and more than one assassin. To admit it, was never part of the plan. Meanwhile, after being accustomed for so many years to the "fourth power of the century" — the communications media — public opinion began to accept that this was a job for the experts. If there was a conspiracy that they didn't want to clear up, it was because it implicitly involved a set of facts that had to be covered up. To solve the mystery, three simple, basic questions must be answered: Who killed Kennedy, how and why?

By 1962 there was already a growing campaign of hostility against Kennedy, as president and as politician, as mentioned by Fidel Castro in his speech two days after the assassination. Certain power groups, unhappy with Kennedy's domestic and foreign policies, arrived at the conclusion that it was necessary to eliminate him and above all impede his reelection and his ability to carry out his reforms. Was there, then, some official meeting where the representatives of these groups decided to assassinate Kennedy and kept a record to that effect? No. Such a meeting never took place. The conspiracy was carried out in the dynamic of the false secret, between the lines, door to door, ear to ear and in the dark, supported by a common objective. It was a process through which every time one addressed another they considered that a third would agree, or perhaps that a fourth would find it practical, but without making clear their intentions; that is, it was not necessary for the agreement to be explicit for it already to be a reality. According to the evidence presented in the previous chapter, there was certainly no lack of powerful people in the United States who might be interested in the political elimination of Kennedy.

But why assassinate him? Because, in certain circumstances the complex mechanisms of U.S. representative democracy end up making political negotiation impractical when faced with the maneuvers of strong interest groups. Parallel or invisible powers such as the Pentagon and the CIA, Pluto and Mongoose, resolve to take matters into their own hands, leading to this type of extreme solution. This practice originated more than a hundred years ago;

Kennedy was not the first U.S. president to be assassinated. There have been three others, including Abraham Lincoln.

There are several possible ways to explain the plot to assassinate Kennedy. There were many tendencies whose only objective was to deflect the blame from the true culprits. The conspiracy began to develop at the end of 1962, in the wake of the Missile Crisis. In the brief period of two years, walking a thin line like a talented tightrope walker between conservative and progressive thinking, before the 1962 crisis the President opted for non-intervention and peaceful coexistence. He earned the visceral hate of "the Tyrians and the Trojans," and the anti-Castro faction for a second time felt definitively betrayed by him. The balance was lost and the death of Kennedy was decided. With a consensus regarding the motive, the next step was to devise a plan, find the right people to carry it out, and the ideal place and time.

Let us stop for a moment at the first level: the assassination itself. On the basis of the information offered by U.S. investigations and the main investigations undertaken by the Cuban State Security Department into the plans to assassinate Fidel Castro directed by the CIA and others, the pieces begin to fall into place and a story develops.

Among the possible authors of the plan to assassinate Kennedy, there are three likely candidates, all possessing the "means and the motives." In the first place, the FBI's J. Edgar Hoover, now dead, the ex-director and a prominent part of the organization, was an intimate of the Truman and Eisenhower cabinets; but he lost power and influence during the Kennedy administration. Hoover, with his facade of incorruptibility, opened the door for the strengthening of the Mafia and the persecution of Blacks. John Kennedy put the brakes on these dvelopments, and placed the FBI under the control of the Justice Department, subject to Attorney General Robert Kennedy. Therefore, Hoover had strong motives and could have participated in the conspiracy, but he was sufficiently adept not to have involved himself directly in the plan of action. The possibility that he could be accused was great and also, within the system of government, it was he and his team who would be in charge of investigating the Kennedy assassination.

Hoover's immunity had to be preserved. Nevertheless, it is important to recall the fundamental role that the FBI played immediately after the assassination, falsifying, nullifying testimony and intimidating witnesses, as well as covering up the story and the links of its agents with Lee Harvey Oswald.

The second possibility: the Mafia. There are two individuals that the Cuban State Security Department followed throughout their investigations: one was Jack Ruby, and the other was Santos Trafficante. Both were originally members of the Chicago Mafia according to written records and through careful observation. In 1947, Jack Ruby formed part of a Mafia contingent that the Chicago "family" sent to the southern United States to expand the drug trade, casinos, and prostitution. Ruby was a low-level Mafia capo who was part of a plan being developed in Texas. Arriving in Dallas, he set up the nightclub that he would own there until 1963, establishing a special relationship with the FBI and the Dallas police, whom he paid off to facilitate his illegal transactions. Santos Trafficante traveled to Cuba at the end of the 1940s. His first trip was as a tourist. He returned twice to that country during the first half of the 1950s. Like Ruby, Trafficante was a small-time Mafia capo, sent for the same reasons by the Chicago family, first to Florida, then to Havana. In 1955 he took up residence in Havana.

In 1948, when Lucky Luciano, the powerful Chicago mafioso, was in Cuba, conversations were held with the government in power at the time — the government of Carlos Prío — to establish the gambling business there. At the meeting in the Appalachian mountains in 1954, the zones of influence were divided up between the principal Mafia capos in Luciano's confidence, among them Joe Colombo, Alberto Anastasia and Meyer Lansky, who later organized their own "families" or changed their patrons. Lansky, considered second in line after Luciano, would become the great Mafia chief of Cuba, backed by Batista and maintaining links with both Jack Ruby in Dallas and Santos Trafficante in Havana. This was the period of the great investments of the Mafia in the hotels and casinos such as the Havana Hilton, the Riviera, the Capri, and others; and the Barlovento Tourist Complex (now Marina Hemingway), a beautiful cove where a ferry arrived daily from

Miami, full of tourists and gamblers. Others came on the frequent flights between Miami and Havana. The complacency of the police authorities guaranteed the success of the Mafia businesses.

At the end of July 1959, when the new revolutionary Cuban authorities confiscated the gambling casinos, Santos Trafficante was arrested and held in Triscornia (an establishment for undesirable foreigners awaiting deportation) until he was finally expelled from the country on August 8. Earlier in the month, according to an English journalist who was also detained there, Santos Trafficante was visited at least once by Jack Ruby. Cuban immigration records show that Ruby was in Cuba twice during August 1959. Once he stayed eight days; the other time, overnight. In Havana he also met with Lewis J. McWilly, a U.S. manager of the Tropicana Cabaret, who later became an important Mafia chief in Las Vegas. Returning to Florida, Trafficante established relations with counter-revolutionary movements; he also participated with them in the narcotrafficking from South America, taking advantage of CIA installations in Guatemala, Costa Rica, Nicaragua and later Panama.

There are many indications that Trafficante was also involved in the Kennedy assassination. As already mentioned in Chapter 1, the 1978 House Committee emphasized that like Carlos Marcello (the leader of the Mafia in Louisiana), Trafficante (the Cosa Nostra boss in Miami) could have been involved in the assassination of John F. Kennedy. Santos Trafficante was one of the principal targets of the energetic measures taken by Robert Kennedy, the Attorney General, against organized crime. The Attorney General's great interest in prosecuting Trafficante occurred at the same time that the CIA officials were using Trafficante's services in their plans to assassinate Fidel Castro, a fact of which Robert Kennedy was unaware.

In testimony before the Committee, Santos Trafficante admitted his participation in the unsuccessful CIA conspiracies to eliminate Castro, arguing that his involvement was motivated by "patriotic" sentiments. Due to the close relations that he maintained with Cubans during the years that he was a Mafia chief in Havana, Santos Trafficante was the "bridge" to the Cuban community in exile. It was he who recruited Cubans to cooperate in the planning and the execution of the attempted Castro assassination. The capsule case is one example: it was through Trafficante that the key man was found, Tony Varona.

The House Committee concluded that the position that Trafficante held with the Cuban exiles could have been fundamental in the conspiracy to assassinate Kennedy. During the course of the investigations, the Committee resolved to check on information published in the *Washington Post* in 1976, whose source was José Alemán Gutiérrez, to the effect that Trafficante had told him in a private conversation in September 1963 that President Kennedy "would be eliminated." According to Alemán, Trafficante told Jimmy Hoffa, head of the Teamsters Union, during the same conversation, that President Kennedy "would get what he had coming to him" as a result of his efforts to prosecute Hoffa. Later, he declared that he had the impression that Trafficante was not the individual who was planning the assassination.

In a Committee hearing in March 1977, José Alemán Gutiérrez supplied more details: in the course of the conversation Trafficante made clear that he knew that the crime was being planned and gave the impression that Hoffa was the principal director of the plan to assassinate Kennedy. Alemán also declared that he relayed the information on Trafficante's alleged comments to FBI agents in 1962 and 1963, but the Committee did not understand why he waited so many years to make public the supposed incident. It was possible, they argued, that the journalist leaked the story, which he later retracted because of death threats, through carelessness or personal vengeance. At that time Alemán had lost the millions of dollars which his father had taken to Cuba, and which were now in the hands of the Mafia.

As in the classic detective stories, the Assassinations Committee reported that organized crime had the motives, the means and the ability to assassinate Kennedy. In that respect we must emphasize: it is one thing to be responsible for an action, and another to carry it out. The brutal style of the Mafia was not capable of developing the plan; but it was instrumental in its execution. One or more of its bosses could have supplied resources, and the sharpshooters could have been recruited from its cadres. With everyone accepting that the Mafia could have been responsible for the crime, the FBI investigations concluded that it was not the author.[58] In this way time passed and nothing was clarified.

The third suspect is the CIA. It is here that the Kennedy assassination, the attempts on Fidel Castro, plans to assassinate other foreign leaders, and the Mafia converge. This was suggested in 1967 by John Roselli, the principal mafioso used by the CIA in its plans to assassinate Castro. In that year Roselli was in the midst of another of his frequent problems with the U.S. Immigration and Naturalization Service, and he was being threatened with deportation. To pressure the government in his favor, he met with journalists Drew Pearson and Jack Anderson and revealed his links with the CIA for the planned killing of Castro.

Without naming his sources, Anderson published the story in his column in the *New York Times* in March 1967, unleashing a series of articles and commentaries on CIA-Mafia plots. Robert Kennedy told advisers that on a certain occasion he learnt of one such plan, but ordered its cancellation. President Johnson asked the CIA to explain. Richard Helms produced the only copy of a memorandum from Colonel Sheffield Edwards, dated May 1962, which said that the planned assassination (capsules — Case 2) had been discontinued some time earlier.

It was the first time that John McCone knew that the Agency had been involved in an assassination plan with the Mafia, but he was satisfied because it had not been initiated during his tenure as director. At that time, not only did the capsule case come out of the security offices through the "covert" hands of William Harvey; but also Helms declined to mention Project AM-LASH (Cubela), which he himself directed — a project which was initiated after McCone assumed the directorship. President Johnson later told a

---

[58] This evidence coincides with that of Mark Lane in his recent book *Plausible denial*. Lane clings to the "sound the retreat" theory: "If the Warren Report were to be completely discredited, those responsible for the death of Kennedy would come up with an alternative theory to protect themselves." According to Lane, "organized crime was a perfect suspect."

journalist: "They were running an operation called Murder Incorporated in the Caribbean."

In July 1971, Roselli was again pursued by the judicial authorities, accused of fraud. A judge decided to sentence him to five years in prison. His lawyers demanded a reduction of the sentence, alleging that their client was a patriot, a kind of Cold War hero, because he had served the nation risking his life to try to eliminate Fidel Castro. In court Roselli delicately declined to respond to questions about his relationship to the CIA, saying that he was sworn to secrecy for reasons of national security. The district attorney insisted that the man represented a menace to society because of his history of extortion and corruption. Their client threatened, Roselli's lawyers looked for journalist Jack Anderson. Roselli made new revelations on the role of the CIA in plans for assassinations, giving facts and names attesting to covert operations. Once again without citing his source, Anderson made public the names of the CIA officials: Jim O'Connell (capsules — Case 1) and William Harvey (capsules — Case 2).

Various episodes about the Agency and organized crime in Miami and Las Vegas were described, one of them involving U.S. millionaire Howard Hughes and his business manager Robert Maheu (the CIA intermediary in the first capsules case). Maheu was presented as the person who recruited John Roselli and was subsequently mobbed by journalists in his Las Vegas office. The press also looked for Harvey, but he refused to make a statement, arguing that since it was such a long story, publishing it would be impractical.

There can be no doubt that Washington had utilized organized crime for assassination operations, links which originated with the collaboration of Lucky Luciano ánd Meyer Lansky with Naval Intelligence in World War II. To alleviate this situation, Richard Helms (by this time director of the Agency), asked his advisers to prepare a report that would highlight the Mafia's participation in the plans.

Then came the Watergate scandal in 1972, and the names surfaced of various Cubans involved with the CIA in counter-revolutionary activities. When they entered the national offices of the Democratic Party on the night of June 17, they claimed to be seeking proof that Senator George McGovern, the Democratic presidential candidate, "was receiving money from Fidel Castro and Ho Chi Minh (the president of North Vietnam) for his political campaign."[59] Bernard Baker, Rolando Eugenio Martínez (Musculito),[60] Virgilio González and Frank Sturgis, wearing surgical gloves and carrying instruments for burglary and telephone interception, were surprised and taken to a Washington jail. The operation was directed by veteran CIA agent Howard Hunt, who served in the White House as an adviser. Another Cuban, named Félix Rodríguez, was also detained for his participation in Watergate[61]; and Rafael Quintero[62] was another Cuban name that came up along with Manuel Artime, due to their close relations to Howard Hunt (the godfather of his children), Frank Sturgis and Rolando Eugenio Martínez. Faced with the path the investigation was taking, exploiting the links between Howard Hunt and the Watergate burglars, Nixon asked his chief of staff, H.R. Haldeman, to alert the top CIA officials (Richard Helms and Vernon Walters)

---

[59] *El Nuevo Herald*, Miami. June 14, 1992.

[60] Rolando Eugenio Martínez, alias "Musculito," was the faithful operative of the naval bases of the Cuban exiles. After the scandal broke, Rolando Martínez declared that he had conducted 300 clandestine missions to infiltrate Cuba, before, during and after Operations Pluto and Mongoose. He became a millionaire in the 1970s, and was hired by Richard Nixon as vice-president of "Keyes Royalty" of Miami, one of the enterprises with state support that featured figures from the Mafia and the Batista government in management positions. The senior CIA official Richard Helms testified before the Watergate Commission that Martínez was a third-rate agent who was occasionally paid something for his services, but in reality Martínez was one of the best paid operatives in Project Cuba.

[61] According to the aforementioned article by Paul Kangas, Félix Rodríguez was directed by George Bush from the time of the Bay of Pigs operation through the Iran-Contra operation. (Source: *Washington Post* July 10, 1990). Tape recordings from the archives on Rodríguez also expose his relationship to Bush. (Source: Project Censored Report. February, 1989. Dr. Carl Jensen. Sonoma State College). According to the Cuban State Security Department, Rodríguez was also involved in the death of Che Guevara in Bolivia in 1967.

[62] Rafael Quintero said publicly that if he were to reveal everything he knew about Dallas and the Bay of Pigs, it would create a huge scandal.

so that they could take the necessary precautions, because the investigations could reopen the whole Bay of Pigs question.[63]

In 1974 it was Robert Maheu who began to break the silence. Howard Hughes fired him, accusing him of being a thief. Maheu stated in court that Hughes did a delicate job for the CIA connected with killing Castro. In May 1975, when Roselli was "retired" and living in Miami, he received a summons to appear before the Senate Intelligence Committee regarding plots to assassinate Castro. According to Senator Frank Church, chairman of the committee, Roselli supplied "a detailed account." Robert Maheu also testified, revealing various aspects of the case. Sam Giancana was also on the list of those cited to appear, but on the night of June 24, a few days before he was scheduled to testify before the committee, someone entered his Chicago residence and shot him in the head with a 22 caliber gun equipped with a silencer. Later the gun showed up on the banks of the Des Plaines River.

The Church Committee announced their hypothetical conclusions regarding the culpability of the Mafia, and did not explore the responsibility of the CIA in the series of plans to assassinate foreign leaders. Both Richard Helms and William Harvey lied, denying their links to the Mafia. Referring to the Mongoose project, Helms himself testified there it was very clear to all that "the desire was to eliminate Castro and his regime, and that there were no limits to this prescription." He also confirmed that, as was customary, without consulting his director John McCone, he authorized the trip to Paris in October 1963 of Desmond FitzGerald (head of the SAS), posing as a representative of the Kennedys, to meet with Cubela. William Harvey now recalled that

---

[63] See Kutler, Stanley I. *The wars of Watergate*. Alfred A. Knopf. New York. 1990. On this subject, there is a tape recording from June 23, 1972, where Nixon can be heard conversing with Haldeman about how to stop the FBI investigation, because it might reveal his connection to the Bay of Pigs invasion. On the tape, Nixon refers to "the Cubans," "the Texans," to Richard Helms, Howard Hunt, Bernardo Baker, Robert Mosbacher, and the Bay of Pigs. After Congress listened to some of these tapes, the Watergate Investigation began holding secret sessions. That was the end of the knowledge about the tapes and also of the inquiry into the Bay of Pigs.

in January 1961 Richard Bissell (during his time as assistant director of "operations") told him that the White House had twice suggested the creation of "executive capabilities" for the elimination of foreign leaders (ZR Rifle), a job for which Harvey was then appointed by Bissell. He added that they preferred not to use the term assassination, but rather "magic button."

After the Church Report was completed, Senator George McGovern was in Cuba and asked for information on the attempts against the Cuban president. He was given an account of the principal cases where the CIA could not hide their responsibility. As a group, these now formed a long chain of possible attempts, of which this book has chosen to highlight only a small portion.[64] On August 7, 1976, after John Roselli insinuated that he knew who planned the assassination of John F. Kennedy, his body was found floating in an oil tank in Dumfounding Bay, on the Florida coast. After Roselli's death, journalist Jack Anderson revealed that Roselli had been the source of his information.

When the House Committee was created in 1978 at the request of George McGovern to investigate the assassinations, the Cuban government also received questionnaires regarding the anti-Cuba operations of the CIA. Announcing the probability of a conspiracy and connecting the Mafia chiefs Trafficante and Marcello to the Kennedy assassination, the committee made little progress. The Agency got the message and wiped out every sign of its participation, protecting all of its fronts. As in so many Hollywood

---

[64] Already in 1956, when Fidel Castro was still in Mexico preparing the expedition on the yacht *Granma* which would land in eastern Cuba, there was a CIA official with this objective around the group. His name was John Maples Spiritto, and he confessed the plan when he was detained in Cuba in 1962. Among all of the persons stalking Castro, Cubela stands out. On February 28, 1966, after a year and a half of investigations, Cubela and his accomplices were arrested in Havana where they had planned an attempt on Castro with a telescopic rifle. Their relationship to the CIA and the groups in Miami was evident, but it was not possible to clarify this once they began to have contact with the Agency. Cuban intelligence was only able to complete its knowledge of the case when it read the U.S. Senate Committee's reports in 1975, which confirmed an operation with the code name AM-LASH. The Cuban State Security Department understood that AM-LASH was Cubela.

films, the events led to murders, federal hearings and trials; in this case, more to confuse than to solve.

The three plans

According to the Cuban State Security Department, the Cubela-Artime plan described in the previous chapter is related to Kennedy's death itself. One of the main conclusions of the Cuban analysts is that there was a plan orchestrated in three parts, beginning at the end of 1962 with the fall out from the Missile Crisis: the murder of Fidel Castro, the murder of Kennedy, and the invasion of Cuba. Two hunts, parallel and simultaneous, and one great pretext.

Let us reconstruct the path of Lee Harvey Oswald, not to contradict the argument that he was the author of the assassination, but rather establishing him from now on as a fabricated suspect and the instrument of a premeditated plan.

By May 1963, Oswald was residing in New Orleans. He had been trained by Military Intelligence at bases in Tokyo and the El Toro Marine Base in California, and then "deserted" to the Soviet Union, where he "revealed" military secrets, and was recruited to play his role in the triple plan referred to earlier.

Part one: New Orleans, the Fair Play for Cuba Committee and DRE episodes — Oswald began to act openly with two objectives: to appear to be an active sympathizer of the Cuban revolution and of Black rights; while at the same time secretly working in an anti-communist organization.

Part two: Dallas, late September, the Silvia Odio-Oswald episode finds him on the side of the anti-Castro forces. One of them, "Leopoldo," informs Silvia that Oswald is a good shot and that he says he must kill Kennedy.

•In the New Orleans-Dallas context, what was the "pro-Cuban" Oswald doing mixed up with the anti-Castro people? How could this Oswald, who showed sympathy for Cuba and Black rights (precisely a feature of Kennedy's policy), have a reason to kill his President? Maneuvering secretly and linked to anti-Castroites and anti-communists, he acts as a provocateur in New Orleans by making pro-Castro propaganda and starting arguments on the streets, alarming public opinion against Kennedy and Castro. Back in Dallas he reappears as an instigator within the MRP, the anti-Castro group with social democratic aspirations, with the same objectives: anti-Kennedy and anti-Castro. How many apparent contradictions! Marxist-Leninist, sympathizer with Cuba, anti-Kennedy and related to the anti-Castroites. But Oswald was neither apparition nor reality; he was simply a "patsy."

Part three: Mexico, September and October. Oswald insists on going to Cuba, saying among other things that he was in the U.S. Communist Party and that he wanted a chance to meet the Cuban leader. But he was not granted a visa.

•The Mexican episode was crucial for incriminating Fidel Castro in the assassination of Kennedy. On the way to Mexico, Lee Harvey Oswald was already the man being prepared for the operation in Dallas. His first visit was to the Cuban Embassy — not to that of the Soviet Union, where he was supposedly going and for which he had other routes available. Instructed to be convincing, he showed various pro-Castro, communist credentials. We emphasize that it was the CIA itself which called attention to an Oswald at the Cuban Embassy, revealing their need to definitively prove this connection, either through a recent trip or through his possession of a visa to be used in the near future. It is enough to remember the confusion created by David Phillips, the head of the Agency in Mexico City, first affirming and then denying the presence of the real Oswald in the Cuban diplomatic mission, which possesses the documents to prove it.

Part four: Dallas, October and November. Oswald takes target practice with a rifle bought by mail order under a pseudonym. On November 22, he is arrested in a movie house, accused of murdering the policeman Tippit and the following day, charged with the assassination of Kennedy. Two days later, Oswald himself is shot by Jack Ruby.

•Why did Oswald go with such determination to the Texas Theater? The conclusion of the Cuban State Security Department is that he was ordered to be in that location, an instruction not unlike most of those he had followed in recent years. Having left a trail as the assassin, Oswald would be eliminated in the movie house, and his body would be left there or in plain sight on some street corner. Whoever was assigned to murder him in the Texas Theater did not arrive on time, or didn't have the sufficient time or courage to act at that moment. And the police unit that received a call from the manager of the store, authorized by a superior who may or may not have been involved in the conspiracy[65] but not in the elimination of Oswald, appeared on the scene first, and arrested him.[66] Let us remember another important date: on this same day Silvia Odio recognized Oswald on television and her "friend" immediately transmitted this information to the FBI. That is how the story of Silvia Odio surfaced in the intimacy of the intelligence agencies. As this last information came in, the structure of the initial plan fell apart completely. So Oswald had to be assassinated by Jack Ruby on Sunday morning, November 24, in the basement of the Dallas Court House and Police Station at the moment he was being led toward a police vehicle, surrounded by 70 guards and handcuffed to a police detective. Jack Ruby, who maintained very good relations with the Dallas police, publicly killed him, "burning the Oswald file" and putting an end to the case without a trial. The Warren Commission was never able to explain how and why Ruby entered that heavily guarded area.

As a whole, the Oswald plan failed and it was not possible to avoid the emergence of ambiguities in future U.S. investigations.

---

[65] It is necessary to clarify the concept of police as employed here. In terms of the security apparatus in general, they could include CIA, FBI, or U.S. Secret Service agents, and federal and local police. To take part in the conspiracy — such as the job of casting suspicion on Oswald — it was only necessary that police authorities of the city be involved. It must also be taken into consideration that many Dallas policemen maintained relations with Guy Banister and Jack Ruby.

[66] Days after the assassination of Kennedy, Jack Martin, a former private detective who worked in Banister's office, revealed to a friend his suspicions that David Ferrie had traveled to Dallas the day of the crime. District Attorney Jim Garrison investigated the trip that Ferrie made by car to Texas that day. He concluded that in Houston, Ferrie's job consisted of waiting at a skating rink while two members of the homicide team could be located. From there he was to have taken them in a biplane to a distant spot, but there were last minute changes in plans. David Ferrie spent all of his time in Houston beside a public phone, making and receiving telephone calls.

From the time of the spontaneous declaration of Silvia Odio to the Warren Commission, Oswald's footprints led in the direction of the anti-Castroites; that is, toward a CIA operation. The Commission entered with its disinformation strategy and tried to erase the traces, but with little success. Other errors in the plan were due to a certain level of improvisation.

The President was in the middle of a political campaign, touring various cities. He had already been in Chicago[67] and in Miami. When Kennedy arrived in Dallas he was offered an armored car, but he rejected it. If he had accepted, the attempt would have been made in another place: Kennedy was marked for assassination.[68] As luck would have it, there was an opportunity in Dallas, but it was not the only one.

On March 12, 1964, Richard Helms met with J. Lee Ranking, the principal adviser to the Warren Commission, and told him that the Commission "had to believe his word [!] . . . that Oswald had not been an agent of the CIA." Jim Garrison's investigations demonstrated that Oswald was an agent contracted by the FBI, number 179, in contact with James Hosty in Dallas and John Quigley in New Orleans. It was Hosty himself who, two and a half hours after Kennedy's body was transferred to Washington, was the first to issue a description of the "suspect in the crime" (which, curiously, coincided with that of Oswald). In 1978, James A. Wilcott, an ex-official of the CIA finance department, declared to the Assassinations Committee that the CIA had recruited Oswald from within the ranks of the armed forces "for the expressed purpose of having him act as a double agent in the USSR." This

[67] According to the Paul Kangas article, in Chicago they could not get Mayor Daley to cooperate.
[68] Many U.S. investigators have also pointed out that there was an indifference on the part of those protecting the President, which added to the creation of the Dallas opportunity. In this respect: 1) Five days before the assassination the FBI office in New Orleans received a telex warning of an attempt on the President in Dallas at the end of the week. This warning was never passed on to the proper authorities. Shortly after the crime, it was transferred to the archives of the office. 2) General Charles Cabell, the assistant director of the CIA, had convinced his brother Earle, the mayor of Dallas, to change the route of the motorcade, making it pass by the grassy knoll and slow down at the curve there.

declaration is interesting, considering that Oswald worked in radar at the Atsugi base in Japan, and that U-2 pilot Francis Gary Powers was shot down just before a scheduled meeting between Eisenhower and Khrushchev.

In 1979, before the same Commission, Helms declared that Clay Shaw, an international businessman from New Orleans, linked to Guy Banister Associates, had worked for the Agency (the Committee's report admitted to links between Shaw, Ferrie and Oswald). Retired CIA agent Victor Marchetti said that Helms expressed alarm on several occasions at Jim Garrison's accusations against Shaw and said that it was necessary to provide a "cover" for the affair. Marchetti said that Helms identified Shaw as a CIA contact in the Ferrie era, as "a contract agent or a contact" for the assassination of Kennedy. In 1975, John Martino, a mafioso and a friend of Roselli, told a Texas businessman (Fred Claasen) that he was a CIA agent and knew about the assassination conspiracy. He said: "The anti-Castro groups were in it together with Oswald. . . . He didn't know who he was working for, didn't know who was directing it. . . . Oswald was going to contact someone in the Texas Theater. . . . They were going to meet there and take him out of the country and later eliminate him. . . . Oswald made a mistake and there was no way to correct it. Ruby had to kill him." Martino died shortly after this conversation; it was only related in 1978 when Claasen was interviewed for the *Dallas Morning News*. Thomas Eli Davis III, who had worked with Ruby in contraband weapons and was also a CIA employee, declared confidentially on two occasions that he had used the name Oswald. Davis died under mysterious circumstances in 1973. It is public and noteworthy information that all of the personalities of the Kennedy case who were involved in aspects of the plan — among them Ferrie, Ruby, Shaw and Banister — are dead.

In conclusion, we should explain the concept of the triple plan referred to above — the murder of Fidel Castro, the murder of Kennedy, and the invasion of Cuba — in terms of the crossed paths of Lee Harvey Oswald, Rolando Cubela and Manuel Artime. The three were players of the (anti-Cuban and anti-communist) strategy developed by the CIA after the "discontinuation" of Operation

Mongoose and the Missile Crisis. Kennedy was turning away from a policy of aggression.

Remember that the Cubela-Artime plan had as its objective the elimination of Fidel Castro and the destabilization of the revolutionary government, creating the conditions for an invasion of Cuba. The fact that it was temporarily halted the moment of the Kennedy assassination was due only to a rule of intelligence operations. When an event of this nature occurs, everything else is temporarily "frozen" to wait for the results. And what were they waiting for? The incrimination of Fidel Castro in the assassination of Kennedy, through the Oswald plan, justifying an invasion of Cuba. This clears up the second level of the conspiracy; and therefore, we repeat: there were two parallel hunts going on simultaneously, with one objective, but they followed no predetermined order.

It is worth mentioning that this analysis is not exhausted with the Oswald-Cubela-Artime intersection. These were the most well-known cases, but the CIA had other alternatives in the three objectives. Since our story is constructed from the point of view of the Cuban State Security Department — and their investigation of the attempts on Fidel Castro and his government — it necessarily leads to the establishment of these connections. Looking at the issue more generally and from the same focus, the contradictions of Kennedy's new policy can be found, along with the breaking point: the Missile Crisis.

"Mr. Cool" and the ZR Rifle

The section of the CIA concerned with the anti-Cuba operations was the area most affected by the changes ordered by Kennedy after the Bay of Pigs debacle. The understanding of the Cuban State Security Department, is that this was the sector that created the plan to assassinate Kennedy[69] through Operation ZR Rifle. This

---

[69] On this point there is an agreement with the general findings of Jim Garrison: "A careful examination certainly eliminates the false sponsors. What remains, as the only plausible sponsor with the motivation and the ability to assassinate the President, is the clandestine action arm of the Central Intelligence Agency."

operation covers all of the ground connected to the crime in Dallas: the links with the Mafia and the Cuban anti-Castro groups and the recruiting of special agents and elite marksmen.

Let us reconsider the formation of ZR Rifle. It was directed initially by Allen Dulles, Richard Bissell and later by Richard Helms. William Harvey was the original organizer of the operation. Complementing the information given in Chapter 2, we can add that in the first months of 1961, Bissell entrusted to Harvey the task of creating ZR Rifle, with the aim of strengthening the leverage over top political leaders who represented obstacles to U.S. power, using assassination as a last resort. In practical terms, it meant gathering information, expanding resources, developing contacts and recruiting assassins. In that sense, the field operated in was the underworld, the intelligence agencies, the Mafia, the groups on the extreme right and the Cuban counterrevolutionaries. However, none of this was new; ZR Rifle simply consolidated an old plan, since assassination projects were already being developed within the CIA. The importance was in the fact that, by structuring and concentrating its mechanisms, the Agency trained itself for future operations of the same type. These were called parallel operations that could be authorized or contracted by others, and those who carried them out would not be functional cadres of the Agency. In this way, those who appeared to be activating them were not CIA officials, or even its agents in the formal sense — unless they worked under pseudonyms — in conformity with the principles of covert action: compartmentalization, invisibility and plausible denial.

The idea of ZR Rifle was born in September 1960 when an attempt was planned against Fidel Castro on the occasion of his visit to the United States to participate in a session of the UN General Assembly.[70] From the very beginning the operation had Cuba as its priority, later adding plans to assassinate other foreign leaders. As noted in Chapter 1, the 1975 U.S. Senate Committee

---

[70] The plan was to eliminate the Cuban leader with a box of exploding cigars. See: Wise, David and Ross, Thomas. *The invisible government*. New York. Random House, 1964.

revealed that there was CIA meddling in the assassinations of Lumumba and Trujillo, although it was not proven that they participated in the actual acts.

At a meeting of the National Security Council on August 18, 1960, then President Eisenhower and his Secretary of State, John Foster Dulles, gave CIA Director Allen Dulles the task of assassinating Patrice Lumumba. According to the testimony of the head of the Agency in the Congo, they began to close in on Lumumba, and several attempts were made, but the plans were never concretized due to the uncontrollable "W.I. Rogue," one of the agents recruited by William Harvey. The Agency then decided to dispatch Joseph Schreider, the head of their laboratories, to the Congo with a kit containing poison in the form of a synthetic botulism. Testifying before the commission, Schreider admitted having given the deadly kit to the head of the Agency in that country. Considering the testimony of CIA officials, the Church Committee concluded that, before they could acquire personal objects of Lumumba in which to deposit the poison, the leader had already been murdered; that in January 1961, during a flight to Bakwanga (Katanga), the plane was diverted to Elizabethville, whose inhabitants were his political enemies and who assassinated him.

In the case of Trujillo, the Dominican dictator that the CIA supported in his first attempt to overthrow the Cuban revolution in 1959, the Senate Committee verified that Richard Bissell, then assistant director of covert operations, had approved on April 7, 1961, the sending of machine guns to conspirators in the Dominican Republic; that in May, shortly after the Bay of Pigs disaster, through the negotiations of the U.S. consul in Ciudad Trujillo, the CIA apparently attempted to convince the group to stop the plan, but by that time it was already too late. President Kennedy learned of the plot and recommended that the CIA back away from it, because the U.S. public would not stand for assassinations. On May 30, 1961, the conspirators stopped Trujillo's car on a highway at the edge of the sea and assassinated him.

It was learned that during 1961, William Harvey traveled to Marseilles in France and recruited another agent (code name Q.J.

Win) who worked on the Lumumba case. One version of the identity of Q.J. Win appears in the House Committee investigations: he was one of the men from the Corse Union, the Marseilles organized crime group, which showed the presence of the Mafia in the plans to assassinate foreign leaders. Q.J. Win met the indispensable requirement of being a Mafioso of non-U.S. origin. Now familiar with the tricks of these manipulators, we can conclude that this was the ideal way of salvaging the "honor" of the North American Mafia.

On the planned attempts against Fidel Castro, we now know that in November 1961, it was Harvey who personally renewed the contacts with Mafia bosses Sam Giancana and John Roselli for the capsule case. As head of the Task Force W of Operation Mongoose, he sent agents on special missions to Cuba with the objective of developing an armed uprising; efforts which, as we can see, fell through. More disastrous was the sequence of events during the Missile Crisis. Someone had to pay for the failure of Mongoose so that the Agency and its high officials — such as assistant director Richard Helms — would be protected. That someone was William Harvey, who already seemed to everyone to be an inconvenient and incompetent drunkard. This being the case, he was fired from the center of anti-Cuba operations in January 1963.

And what happened to ZR Rifle? It was taken over by no less than David Atlee Phillips, who at the same time was moving toward the extreme right. Phillips was extremely adept at social communication. He was a great "counterintelligence" strategist, an expert in "psychological warfare." His background, before the Kennedy assassination, included several covert actions in Chile (1952), in Guatemala (1954) and in Havana (1958-59-60); coordinating the area of "counterintelligence" in the Cuban plan (1960-61-62); and being CIA station chief in Mexico (1963). Analyzing the evidence of Antonio Veciana about his famous case official, "Maurice Bishop," the Cuban State Security Department arrived at the conclusion that this was the code name of David Phillips. In Havana it was Phillips who recruited Veciana, introducing himself as "Bishop." One proof that Phillips was residing in that city is contained in information about U.S. citizens residing in Cuba in 1960, which appeared in a guide published by Texaco and distributed in Havana: "David Atlee Phillips, nationality: United States; wife: Helen Florence Haash; children, Maria, David, Atlee and Christopher; position in the U.S. embassy in Cuba in 1959: Public Relations Consultant; proprietor of 'David Atlee Phillips Associates,' located at 106 Humboldt St., apartment 502, telephone 70-00-16; residence: 21413 Avenue 19 A, Nuevo Baltimore, Marianao; member of the American Club, and his wife of the Mothers." There is a note from the same era, on a paper stamped by the Havana Chamber of Commerce, which reads: "David A. Phillips Associates. The only press agency in Cuba specializing in the interior of the republic, 106 Humboldt St., apartment 502, telephone 70-00-16."[71]

From this point, all of Veciana's comings and goings would be marked by the presence of Phillips, his supervisor in all his anti-Castro activities. In 1961, he guided him in the Operation Liborio attempt on Fidel Castro. In 1962, by suggesting to him the creation of Alpha 66, Phillips unleashed a series of terrorist groups. Phillips directed the beginning of the Alpha 66 attacks. These intensified during the Missile Crisis, trying to provoke a political confrontation with President Kennedy. Phillips told Veciana that the terrorist activities were aimed at forcing. Kennedy to take a position against Cuba. In 1963, with the Miami camps being dismantled by the police authorities and some of the best commandos relocated to Central America, it was necessary to reunify them. The man chosen for this job was David Phillips, because of his long association with these groups.

---

[71] In the middle of 1958, David Phillips was the agent expressly recommended by the CIA headquarters to its Inspector General Lymon Kirkpatrick, to serve as a special consultant during his visit to Havana, the objective of which was to learn of the dimensions of the social and political movement that was about to overthrow the Batista regime. The meeting between Kirkpatrick and Phillips was held in the Berlitz language school, located on 23rd Avenue in the Vedado neighborhood. The footsteps of "Bishop" and the Berlitz academy were followed by Gaetón Fonzi (op. cit.), who tried, unsuccessfully, to confirm the identity of Phillips.

Lastly, at this time, where could the necessary capacities for ZR Rifle be found, such as the resources of big business, the Mafia, the anti-Castro groups or the best marksmen? In the terrorist groups. The fact that this was Phillips' new job can be confirmed through the testimony of Veciana: he saw in "Bishop's" folder a memorandum bearing the initials "to H.H." which confirmed commando plans, contacts and activities. (H.H. could have been either Howard Hunt or Howard Hughes, Robert Maheu's boss in Las Vegas and head of the commercial activities of the CIA). In September 1963, Veciana again witnessed an encounter between Phillips and Lee Harvey Oswald in Dallas. Oswald was on his way to Mexico and Phillips was already the CIA's man in that country. After the episode, Veciana recalled that Phillips ("Bishop") asked him to go to Mexico and look up his cousin's husband Guillermo Ruíz (the G-2 agent), who at that time was stationed there. Phillips proposed that Veciana offer Ruíz a large sum of money to desert and testify to Oswald's visit to the Cuban embassy and his pro-Castro affiliation.

The House Assassinations Committee heard two testimonies which shed a ray of light on the participants in the Kennedy assassination. The first was that of José Alemán, already related here, which implicated Santos Trafficante in the crime and suggested that three Cubans served as marksmen. The other was that of Marita Lorenz, a beautiful spy recruited by Frank Sturgis in mid-1959, when she maintained relations with people close to Fidel Castro. Lorenz mentioned an encounter she witnessed in Miami in September 1963, at the home of Orlando Bosch where Pedro Luís Díaz Lanz and Lee Harvey Oswald — whom she had seen earlier in an Operation 40 house — were present. The conversation revolved around a trip to Dallas. She said that on November 15, she was part of a group which drove to that city in two cars, and which included Bosch, Frank Sturgis, Díaz Lanz, Oswald, Gerry Hemmings and the Novo Sampol brothers (Guillermo and Ignacio, from the Movimiento Nacionalista Cubano — Cuban Nationalist Movement). They stayed at a hotel in rooms containing various rifles and shotguns, and Jack Ruby paid them a visit there. Lorenz said that she returned to Miami on November 19 or 20. She also said that she had been coerced by Sturgis not to testify before the Committee, which ended up judging her statements inconsistent anyway. Nevertheless, the Cuban State Security Department considered the evidence of Marita Lorenz to be important.

Following the reasoning of the Cuban State Security, we conclude that the Kennedy case involves apparently juxtaposed groupings:

• *The counterintelligence* — Frank Sturgis and Orlando Bosch were two of the principal agents of Operation 40, the "parallel" counterintelligence structure before, during and after the Bay of Pigs invasion. David Atlee Phillips represented the CIA in these operations.

• *The commandos* — Sturgis was one of the initiators of the International Anti-Communist Brigades, along with Díaz Lanz, who was in charge of training the elite troops in exile. David Atlee Phillips was the mentor of these terrorist groups. Sturgis and his partner Gerry Hemmings opened the training camp at Lake Pontchartrain in New Orleans in the same era as the creation of Alpha 66. Orlando Bosch was the head of the MIRR, one of the most important terrorist groups trained at Lake Pontchartrain.

• *The Mafia* — the arms at Pontchartrain were supplied with the cooperation of the Mafia. The Louisiana corridor was controlled in Dallas by Jack Ruby, and in Miami by Santos Trafficante. Sturgis had been involved in the contraband arms trade since before the 1959 Cuban revolution. Trafficante was the bridge between the Mafia and the Cuban exiles.

The month of August 1963 was the time; and New Orleans, the place. All of the Florida training camps had been liquidated by government order. Pontchartrain, spared by the police authorities, became the center of the illegal counterrevolutionary operations. Frank Sturgis, Orlando Bosch, Guy Banister, David Ferrie, Clay Shaw and Lee Harvey Oswald all participated directly in these. Later, New Orleans became the center for the parallel operation of the CIA. It was in the beginning of August that, due to growing pressure from Kennedy, the FBI was obliged to reveal the secret of Pontchartrain.

The ultra right understood that the Kennedy government would in no way accept this parallel operation. The CIA had the ideal man in their hands: Lee Harvey Oswald. At this moment, Oswald was chosen to be accused of the Kennedy assassination, an instrument of the triple plan. On August 9 while distributing pro-Castro literature printed in the Banister office he was confronted on the streets of New Orleans by Carlos Bringuer, the leader of the DRE. It was also in August that, according to José Alemán Gutiérrez's testimony, Santos Trafficante had the conversation about the Kennedy assassination. In the two months that followed, September and October, we see David Atlee Phillips directing Oswald's steps in Dallas and Mexico. And Phillips was the head of ZR Rifle, the source of parallel operations for political assassinations.

Some events prior to the Kennedy assassination serve to reinforce this argument. Frank Sturgis provided a fundamental piece of the disinformation machinery as spokesperson for the theory that Fidel Castro was responsible for the Kennedy assassination,[72] spreading information that Oswald was in contact with Cuban intelligence in Mexico and New Orleans. Also, David Phillips had already begun his tour of other Latin American countries at the end of 1963, setting things up with the commando terrorists[73] he would work with in the Dominican Republic in the 1965 invasion; and directing Veciana's steps in Bolivia from 1968 until 1972. He hatched the "Track-2" plot, the attempt on the Chilean General René Schneider in 1970, mentioned in the Senate Committee hearings in 1975, and developed the planned attempt on Fidel Castro in October 1971, also in Chile.

---

[72] See Fonzi, Gaetón. Op. cit. The afternoon that Senator Schweiker's report was published, Sturgis told Fonzi that he had attended a meeting in Havana two months prior to the assassination of Kennedy, where a group of important people, including Jack Ruby and Cuban leaders Fidel Castro, Raúl Castro and Che Guevara were working on the conspiracy to assassinate the United States President.

[73] The terrorist groups would be transformed into the extraofficial arms of the Agency to pursue its counterrevolutionary operations, augmented through traditional channels and independent of the greater or lesser support of the U.S. authorities. They would also be directly linked to the international drug trade.

Veciana and Gerry Hemmings were involved in this later attempt on Castro's life. The Cuban President was to be assassinated with a camera-revolver at a press conference after his arrival in Santiago, Chile. According to Veciana, Phillips ("Bishop") set up the operation "in a similar way to the assassination of Kennedy:" the executioner would be carrying papers and documents that would make it appear that he was an agent of Moscow and Castro who had betrayed him. These papers would be supplied by Luís Posada Carriles, an ex-official of the repressive forces of Batista and a known associate of Orlando Bosch. The executioner was to be assassinated immediately after the attempt.

Phillips retired in 1975, when he was still head of the Western Hemisphere branch of the CIA. Afraid of the possibility that Phillips would fall into the hands of the Church Commission, the Agency arranged his rapid separation. This explains why there is no reference to his name or activities in the Commission's report.

Let's get to the final conclusions. The Cuban State Security Department has concluded that those responsible for Kennedy's assassination are David Phillips, as the promoter of ZR Rifle; and Santos Trafficante, as the coordinator of the Mafia participation in the operation. And those who fired the shots were Cubans from the "elite troops" in exile.[74] The day of the assassination they were deployed in groups, together or separate, forming a triangle of fire, and one of these groups was under the direct orders of Jack Ruby. And who was the ultimate author of this entire scheme? Richard Helms, the brain of the CIA.

Helms was the ultimate chief of the covert and parallel operations from the beginning of Operation Mongoose. He was the

---

[74] This evidence coincides with the reasoning of Jim Garrison: "It seemed clear that other persons had fired from both the elevation situated in front of the President and the book depository beside him. . . . The frequent appearances of 'dark skinned' men, 'apparently hispanic' or 'negroes' has me intrigued. This description reminded me of the Cuban exiles who lived out of Banister's office, when they were not receiving guerilla training at Lake Pontchartrain. It occurred to me that the dark skinned man seen by so many witnesses could have been a Cuban. The Cubans began to appear as more probable suspects than Oswald himself."

director of the plans which included the capsules, the special missions, the terrorist commandos, the Mafia, the Banister unit, Pontchartrain, William Harvey, Manuel Artime, Rolando Cubela, Desmond FitzGerald, Lee Harvey Oswald, Santos Trafficante, David Atlee Phillips, and ZR Rifle. He was the conductor of the invisible government and the maestro of plausible denial. Finally, he was the link of the Agency with the "hardliners" and the mentor of the provocations during the Kennedy administration. But Helms' involvement was not apparent; he was behind four walls, an invisible man.

After the assassination, Helms was named director of the CIA. He directed the "Phoenix" program in Vietnam, the systematic assassination of persons suspected of belonging to the Viet Cong. One of those named in the Watergate scandal, he was made ambassador to Iran. Currently he is a business consultant. He is tall, with fine black thinning hair. He is discreet and evasive; the perfect bureaucrat. He is considered the most astute and the coldest of all of the directors of the Agency — so cold that he was nicknamed "Mr. Cool."

Helms, Phillips and Trafficante equals counterintelligence, Mafia and commandos equals Operation ZR Rifle. The equation is solved. But it's not yet the time for euphoria. We are only at the beginning.

CHAPTER 7

Tying up the loose ends

Central Havana. A storm hits the city, like the one in Rio de Janeiro back when all of the questions swirled around in my head. Ahead, the Kennedy case. A labyrinth and a long spiral of countless circles. Clearly, nothing is like it was before, but destiny always returns us to the beginning of the story. Now crossing the finish line, who do I see? The one who opened the doors for me: General Fabián Escalante Font, our Z.[75]

I had already accustomed myself to his sudden disappearances down some shortcut in the road, asking me for "time." In a mysterious way, like everything up until now, each of his returns meant something new was about to be revealed. From Z, through a common ally, I learned that I was on the right path. At that moment he helped me "join the dots" and enabled me to conclude the "final" chapter — the previous one — which in the end would

---

[75] Fabián Escalante, 52 years old, conducted various investigations and operations designed to break up CIA plans and subversive activities against Cuba. According to what he could ascertain, the same people who at certain times participated in these plans were also involved in the workings of the assassination of John F. Kennedy. In 1963, Escalante was in charge of the Cuban counterintelligence units concerned with the fight against the counter-revolutionary organizations. From 1976 to 1982 he was the head of the Cuban State Security Department (or G2). He has become Cuba's expert on the assassination of Kennedy, familiarizing himself with all of the published bibliography on the subject as well as public and private investigations concerning the case. In 1978 Escalante directed a special Cuban investigation in response to a request for assistance from the U.S. congressional committee examining the Kennedy assassination.

be no more than a sweet illusion. Days later more "important news" appeared. This announcement understandably set me back on the road. Pages written, endless editing, an eternal return to the beginning, the middle and the end, like an octopus and its tentacles. Deep in the drama and eager for news, I prepared to solve the final puzzle and "tie up all the loose ends."

Claudia Furiati: Who, in your judgement, are the persons responsible, the ones who planned the assassination of President Kennedy?
Fabián Escalante: As I have told you on various occasions, many of those who have investigated this case, including ourselves, have reached similar conclusions. The CIA, in the person of the heads of the groups which acted against Cuba, the Mafia, and the Cuban counterrevolutionaries were those who were responsible for, planned and carried out the assassination.

Claudia Furiati: Let's start with the counterrevolutionary connection. Are there names, details?
Fabián Escalante: Yes. There is a name that appears in various United States investigations — such as that of the Senate Committee (in 1975) and that of the House (in 1978). That is Manuel Antonio de Varona Loredo — Tony Varona, who since 1960 was a top secret agent of the Mafia and the CIA in various assassination plots against Fidel Castro.

Claudia Furiati: What led you to that conclusion?
Fabián Escalante: As you know, the investigation processes are a labyrinth, they don't follow any fixed rules. Motivated by your investigation, I was reviewing some old files and also some of the extensive bibliography on the Kennedy case. Tony Varona appeared as **Mr. X** in the Senate and House reports. He and his collaborators were tied in with the anti-Cuba conspiracy: they were the planners par excellence of the subversive and criminal activities of the early years. Varona was the man who had been frustrated in his pretensions of being chosen by the United States as the president of post-revolutionary Cuba. Varona was the CIA man,

Richard Helms' and David Phillips' man. An associate of Meyer Lansky and Santos Trafficante. It was Varona who took over the reins of what was left of the Cuban Revolutionary Council when Miró Cardona relinquished them. Varona, who together with Carlos Prío manipulated a group of terrorists who were trained in the camps of Lake Ponchartrain. Varona, among whose collaborators could be found Eladio del Valle, who was savagely assassinated on the same day as David Ferrie.

Claudia Furiati: Any other Cubans?

Fabián Escalante: Yes. Antonio Veciana, head of Alpha 66, a CIA agent since 1960, the organizer of various attempts against Fidel Castro, the head of the most active counterrevolutionary cell in Dallas in 1963, and the participant in a very strange encounter with Lee Harvey Oswald, weeks before the assassination. He was the relative of a diplomat at our embassy in Mexico whom the CIA tried unsuccessfully to recruit, and an active participant in CIA operations in Venezuela, Bolivia and Chile during the decades of the 1960s and the 1970s. Later others will appear, such as Orlando Bosch, the Novo Sampol brothers, Pedro Luís Díaz Lanz, "Tony" Cuesta and several more.

Claudia Furiati: Are there tracks left by some Cuban who might have been a marksman in Dealey Plaza?

Fabián Escalante: In the investigations of District Attorney Jim Garrison, one of the first to investigate the assassination of JFK, the Cuban Eladio del Valle, alias Yito, is mentioned. Yito del Valle was brutally murdered on the same day that David Ferrie died in mysterious circumstances — on the eve of testifying about his participation in the Dallas assassination. Yito del Valle has an extensive record in our files. A former parliamentarian in the Batista era, he was also an agent of the Military Intelligence Service during the dictatorship. He was a partner of Santos Trafficante in smuggling operations in the pre-revolutionary years. He fled to the United States on January 1, 1959. Immediately after he arrived in exile, he joined the conspiracies of Carlos Prío and Tony Varona —

who were associated with David Ferrie, the pilot they used for their subversive expeditions against Cuba.

The investigations of Yito take us to Santos Trafficante, where we encounter one of his henchmen and buddies, an old Cuban gangster, Herminio Díaz García. This character was involved in an anti-government conspiracy in Havana up until going into exile at the end of 1962. Connected with Polita Grau and the "Rescate" group, he was in all probability linked to the episode of the poisoned capsules.

Another of those accused of involvement in the Dallas assassination, Richard Cain of the Chicago Mafia and a CIA agent in Operation Mongoose, visited Havana in October 1960 — precisely the date in which the Mafia sent an emissary to Cuba in order to coordinate the plans to assassinate Fidel. These assassination plans were initiated by the CIA to be carried out by Tony Varona and his "Rescate" group in our capital. Herminio Díaz was also linked with this group.

The criminal record of Herminio Díaz is extensive. A paid assassin for the dictator Trujillo, in 1948 he murdered in Mexico a Cuban named Rogelio Hernández, from whom he took the victim's surname as a pseudonym. In 1957, again under the orders of Trujillo, he attempted to murder the president of Costa Rica, José Figueres. He was subsequently detained in that country.

Both Yito del Valle and Herminio Díaz were expert shooters. If you carefully check the descriptions given by witnesses of the Dallas crime, gathered together by Garrison as well as the Warren Commission, you are going to find that four people mentioned having seen in the book depository "two Latinos or Cubans, one of them black, with an unmistakable bald patch on their heads."

These descriptions correspond to Herminio, who was mulato, and Yito del Valle, who was white but with a dark complexion. Both had unmistakable bald patches.

One of these witnesses, an assistant police officer named Roger Craig, later gave evidence that while outside the book depository building he watched when police unsuccessfully interrogated a Latino or Cuban. Frustrated because the man didn't know English, he was allowed to leave.

A few minutes later, continued Craig, he saw the same Latino, and now focusing his attention on him, described him "not as a dark-skinned man, but like that of a negro." The Latino was now at the steering wheel of a Nash Rambler van stopped at the side of the book depository. A young white man got into the vehicle and they drove away. Craig later identified the young man as Oswald.

All this permits us to conclude that Cuban agents of the CIA — Herminio Díaz and Eladio del Valle — participated in the assassination of Kennedy.

Later, on May 29, 1966, Herminio died in a battle with a Cuban militia patrol while trying to infiltrate the area around the Hotel Comodoro in Havana. He undertook this mission, directed by Jorge Mas Canosa, now the president of the Cuban American National Foundation in the United States, in order to carry out a new attempt to assassinate Fidel Castro. Herminio Díaz was a sought-after paid assassin with important masters, involved in various plans against presidents.

Yito del Valle was brutally murdered in February 1967, in the period in which District Attorney Garrison initiated his investigation into the death of Kennedy.

Claudia Furiati: Who was involved on the part of the Mafia?
Fabián Escalante: They were the same people who have already been mentioned in some way: Santos Trafficante, Sam Giancana, John Roselli and certainly Carlos Marcello and Jimmy Hoffa.

Claudia Furiati: Why certainly?
Fabián Escalante: Because the planning was carried out in Marcello's territory, in addition to the motives that he had. The same was true of Hoffa; he was a mafioso who hated the Kennedys and he undoubtedly knew what was being planned because of his connections to Trafficante. Nevertheless, these speculations are based solely on the investigations carried out in the United States.

The book *Double Cross* by Chuck Giancana, brother of the head of the Mafia in Chicago and a friend of Trafficante, and who was murdered days before testifying at the Church Commission in 1975, allows us to bring together a series of dispersed elements. It confirms that the assassination was planned in the spring of 1963 in New Orleans, and that those responsible were: Roselli, representing the Mafia; General Cabell, the former deputy chief of the CIA; Frank Sturgis, CIA agent and linked to Carlos Prío; Gerry Hemmings; and other high officials of the Agency, especially those who headed the Agency's special operations. As it happens, this was the speciality of David Phillips and Howard Hunt.

It is interesting to observe, following the details given in *Double Cross*, that the assassination of Kennedy was carried out by two groups: one under the control of Jack Ruby, who later killed Oswald; and the other by Frank Sturgis, who later became the chief of the Watergate "plumbers." It's now possible to appreciate why Richard Nixon didn't want the famous phone tapes about the Bay of Pigs to become known.

Claudia Furiati: Who would the others be who helped plan the conspiracy?
Fabián Escalante: On the part of the CIA, the official David Atlee Phillips, who later became chief of the Western Hemisphere division, certainly due to his position at the head of the anti-Cuba group in the early 1960s. Also his boss, Richard Helms, the supervisor of the anti-Cuba operations, who hid from the CIA director of that era, John McCone, the plans to assassinate Fidel Castro with the complicity of the Mafia. Helms disinformed the Congressional commissions on Clay Shaw's connections to the CIA; he organized the operation against the Allende government; he promoted Phillips; and was CIA chief at the time of JM Wave — the great operating base of the CIA in Miami — and the SAS (Special Affairs Service, formerly Task Force W), headed by Desmond FitzGerald. Helms was also CIA chief at the time of the Watergate operation.

Claudia Furiati: Are there other revelations?
Fabián Escalante: Yes. I think that it is very important for history that you are committed to telling this story, to highlighting the CIA official David Phillips, whose trail we've been following for several years. In 1958 he arrived in Cuba as an official without a

diplomatic cover. He worked out of his private office in the City of Havana — David Phillips Associates — and he was charged with penetrating the cultural sector. Later, in 1959, he became the ideal official to coordinate the counterrevolutionary groups, because he had few links with the U.S. Embassy. In 1960 he left Cuba for Miami and there he joined Operation Pluto as head of propaganda — that is, of psychological warfare. In 1962 he was an important operative of Mongoose. The following year he was sent to Mexico to run the anti-Cuba operations, and that's where he was at the time of the assassination of John F. Kennedy. In 1965 he participated in the U.S. operation against Santo Domingo, and later he traveled throughout Latin America organizing counter-insurgency operations. In 1967, when Ernesto Che Guevara was assassinated in Bolivia, he was in charge of the CIA anti-Cuba operations on the continent. In 1971 he was the organizer of the attempt against Fidel Castro's life in Chile, and two years later he participated in the overthrow of President Allende.

Claudia Furiati: Did you ever see him?
Fabián Escalante: No.

Claudia Furiati: Who did see him?
Fabián Escalante: Many people in Cuba. We have information from agents who operated in the anti-Cuba network in the "Phillips Period." It is very difficult to document covert actions. That is the business of shadows — where they use false passports, identities and moustaches along with false names and addresses.

Claudia Furiati: Is any of this information contained in the U.S. investigations?
Fabián Escalante: Exactly. In Gaetón Fonzi's investigation a CIA official appears whom Veciana calls "Maurice Bishop," who is curiously related to Phillips through a chain of events. In the testimony offered by Veciana, he mentioned that he was recruited by "Bishop" in Havana, and that he received training at a place near the Berlitz Language Academy, one of the few clients of David Phillips Associates; and that he was with "Bishop" until the end of

1960 when the latter announced he was leaving Cuba, but later reinfiltrated the island in September 1961, to direct him in a plan to assassinate Fidel Castro. After the crime in Dallas, Veciana recognized the individual he had met in the company of "Bishop" at a meeting place in that city in September 1963 as Lee Oswald. He also stated that on this occasion he did not communicate with Oswald, who left a few minutes after his arrival. But how strange. Having worked in security as many years as "Bishop," I know that it is an inviolable rule not to set up encounters with different agents in the same place unless they have to be present to work together. Let us add another piece of information: several days after the murders of Kennedy and Oswald, even after the Johnson administration refused to blame the Soviet Union and Cuba, Veciana said that "Bishop" tried to persuade him to travel to Mexico to propose to Guillermo Ruiz, an official at the Cuban Embassy, that he defect and confirm that Oswald was a Cuban intelligence agent. Re-analyzing this information we discovered something: evidently the encounter between Oswald and Veciana in Dallas was not casual, it was premeditated and its objective was that Oswald knew the details of the plan to recruit Guillermo Ruiz, so that the latter might serve as support in the Cuban Embassy in Mexico. In that way Veciana was not just a simple spectator, but in reality he was part of the operation to blame Cuba for the assassination of John F. Kennedy.

Gaetón Fonzi offers us yet another element that should not be underestimated: in the description which Veciana gave of "Bishop," Senator Richard Schweiker identified David Phillips. Later the House Committee arranged a meeting between Phillips and Veciana, at which, as could be predicted, they did not recognize each other.

Claudia Furiati: Where is the proof of all this? You referred earlier to the reports of Cuban agents in the CIA network?
Fabián Escalante: There are two other persons who also lead us to David Phillips. The first is "Harold Bishop," the official who unleashed "Operation Peter Pan," the person referred to earlier as a specialist in "psychological warfare," like Phillips. Coincidentally,

with the same last name and with the same description as the CIA official who interviewed the agent José Pujals Mederos in July 1961 in the United States. "Operation Patty" had already failed and "Harold Bishop" ordered Pujals to infiltrate Cuba to transmit instructions to Antonio Veciana — Phillips' agent — and unleash "Liborio." From Veciana's statements to Fonzi, we concluded "Maurice Bishop" was the one who infiltrated Cuba with the same objectives. Therefore "Maurice Bishop" and "Harold Bishop" are the same person and their backgrounds are the same as that of David Phillips. The other person who leads us to Phillips is a CIA official called "Harold Benson," whom we knew in 1968.

Claudia Furiati: Who knew him?

Fabián Escalante: We did. In 1967, the last remnants of the counterrevolution in Cuba were wiped out, and our security organs decided to adapt themselves to the new lines of the CIA; to penetrate their networks and impede their plans for Cuba. Several comrades were prepared outside the country for this task. One of these was Nicolás Sirgado Ross — agent "Noel" for us and "Sapphire" for the CIA — a man very well-placed in the Cuban government. His first trip was to Montreal as a foreign commerce official, and we made sure that the CIA had advance information. In that city he was contacted by a U.S. official who tried to recruit him. Afterwards, "Noel" went on to London. Thanks to other foreseen maneuvers, in February 1968 another veteran CIA official appeared. Nicolás asked what was the objective of the collaboration he wanted to establish, since what was important for us was to know what was behind the CIA operation. From the first moment, it was clear that information on Fidel Castro was the main objective. The official said he was called "Harold Benson" and that he was the head of the CIA's anti-Cuba group in Latin America. According to "Noel's" description, the agent was about 45 years old, gray haired, tall, pleasant, with large teeth and a frank smile, with fluent Spanish and a roguish face. Our agent was also a likable and intelligent person, which facilitated the establishment of a friendly relationship between the two for more than 10 years. Several times I had been struck with the idea that David Phillips could be "Harold Benson." There were many coinciding points in the four records — those of Maurice and Harold Bishop, Harold Benson and David Phillips.

In relation to your investigation, the idea recently occurred to me to interview various agents of that period, so that they might recall who were the CIA officials and what were their respective characteristics. I took the step of bringing with me several photographs, among which was that of David Phillips. It was "Noel" who gave me the overwhelming response, recognizing "Harold Benson" in the photo of Phillips. On that occasion we also recalled another detail: "Benson" used a pipe that he never lit, and on it was a silver plaque with two initials in Gothic letters, which could be interpreted as "HB" or "MB." From his good memory, "Noel" drew these initials for me, and we deduced that the Gothic "H" was an "M". Then the dark was illuminated because it was proven that Benson was Phillips, and surely also Maurice and Harold Bishop.

Let us go on to another detail: in 1973, when another CIA official (Mike) introduced himself to "Noel," he informed him that the change was due to Benson's being promoted to head of the Western Hemisphere division. In mid-1976, months before the crime against the Cuban airplane in Barbados,[76] the CIA was insistently asking "Noel" if Fidel Castro intended to fly to Luanda on November 11, to participate in the commemoration of the first anniversary of the Angolan revolution. He also wanted to know what the Cuban reaction was to the repeated terrorist attacks that were being carried out on Cuban installations outside the country. This was one of the reasons that made President Fidel Castro decide to reveal the "Noel" case at a memorial service for the victims of the Cuban plane bombing,[77] letting the world know of the CIA responsibility for these acts.

---

[76] This crime occurred during the first few days of October 1976, when two CIA agents of Venezuelan nationality, acting under orders of Orlando Bosch and Luís Posada Carriles, placed a bomb on a Cuban airliner which exploded on takeoff from the Barbados airport, killing 76 persons.

[77] Fragments of the speech of President Castro: "We suspect that the government of the United States has not renounced such practices. On October

Claudia Furiati: And what is the connection between the Cuban counterrevolutionaries, the CIA, the Mafia, David Phillips and ZR Rifle in the assassination of Kennedy?

Fabián Escalante: "Operation 40." It underwent a metamorphosis and could even have taken on other names, but its basic functions have endured up to the present. One of the first features of this transformation was after the defeat at the Bay of Pigs, when various groups of "specialists" in assassinations and subversion temporarily had no functions. They represented basically five sectors: the first, were the "secret police" of the mercenary brigade; the second, were those who came out of Nino Díaz's detachment trained at Ponchartrain; the third, were the special missions people prepared in Panama; the fourth, was made up of members of the terrorist groups — the MIRR, Alpha 66, the DRE, the L Commandos, etc.; and the fifth, were the assassins contracted for ZR Rifle, who constituted the connection with the Mafia (John Roselli, Santos Trafficante, Carlos Marcello and Sam Giancana).

These sectors began a process of fusion at the end of 1962, making up a "new" Operation 40. The figures who stand out the most in this phase are the Cubans Joaquín Sanjenís, Díaz Lanz, Félix Rodríguez, Nino Díaz, Manuel Artime, Orlando Bosch, Luís Posada Carriles, Tony Cuesta and others; and the North Americans David Phillips, Howard Hunt, Gerry Hemmings, Frank Sturgis and Clay Shaw. Also, one of the notable pupils of Nino Díaz was

---

6, only three days before the criminal attack in Barbados, a message sent by the CIA to one of its agents in Havana was intercepted. It says, among other things, and I quote, 'Please inform us at the first opportunity of any data with respect to Fidel's attendance at the ceremony of the first anniversary of Angolan independence on November 11. In the affirmative case, try to find out the complete itinerary of Fidel's visit to other countries on the same trip.' Another instruction from an earlier date reads, 'What is the official and private reaction to bomb attacks against Cuban offices abroad? What are they going to do to avoid them and prevent them? Who do they suspect is responsible? Will there be reprisals?' We hope that the government of the United States will not dare to deny the veracity of these instructions from the CIA. . . . In this concrete case, the supposed agent recruited by the CIA, from the very first moment and over 10 years has kept the Cuban government informed in detail of all of its contacts with the CIA, its teams, and the instructions received."

starting out on his political career. This was Jorge Mas Canosa,[78] who would be converted almost overnight into a powerful economic potentate thanks to the drug trade and other illegal activities. The "new" Operation 40 became the invisible arm of the CIA, detached from it only in appearance, directing the terrorism unleashed from 1962 on. It is the "Murder Corporation" of the 1960s to which ex-President Lyndon Johnson referred in a conversation with a U.S. journalist.

Claudia Furiati: Why, in your point of view, was Oswald selected to be accused of the Kennedy assassination?
Fabián Escalante: I don't think he was condemned to death from the very first moment. When Oswald arrived in Dallas from the Soviet Union, he was a CIA or Naval Intelligence agent who was out of work. Because of his background, he was the ideal person. The FBI recruited him to infiltrate the colony of Russian immigrants in Dallas. Later it was necessary to learn about the conspiratorial schemes of Guy Banister and his "Democratic Cuba," and Oswald was sent to New Orleans. Here the rivalry between the FBI and the CIA must be taken into account: the latter, with its Cuban operatives, was carrying out counter-intelligence work in U.S. territory. In New Orleans, in April and May 1963, Oswald's primary activity in the Banister unit was as

---

[78] Mas Canosa went into exile in the United States in 1960. After the Bay of Pigs failure, he joined a special missions and intelligence group that was training at Fort Benning. In 1961, he was secretary of the DRE organization. During that decade, through his links with Operation 40, he began to get rich in the contraband business, taking advantage of the air transportation which existed between the United States and its Central American bases. In the 1970s he began to get involved in U.S. politics as a collaborator of the Republican Congresswoman Paula Hawkins. In 1981, Richard Allen, then National Security Adviser, included him in the project to create the CANF (Fundación Nacional Cubano-Americano — Cuban-American National Foundation), aimed at influencing Congress and public opinion on Cuba, Nicaragua and El Salvador. The CANF was part of the "program for public democracy" directed by William Casey, the CIA chief at the time. The organization would not only play a propaganda role, it took part in the covert operations that Oliver North directed against Central America, and thus became the public face of Operation 40.

David Ferrie's assistant in the traffic of weapons for Ponchartrain. Banister also realized that Oswald was the perfect person to set up a pro-Castro front.

It was around the same time that Miró Cardona resigned from the Cuban Revolutionary Council, when the top counter-revolutionary leaders and their manipulators — the CIA and the Mafia — perceived that Kennedy's plans were clearly not directed toward a military confrontation with Cuba, and they decided to eliminate him. In New Orleans the details of this covert plan were put together under the supervision of three key people — David Phillips, Tony Varona and Santos Trafficante. Oswald's task was to find a way to implicate Cuba in the assassination. In reality there were two conspiracies: the one to murder Kennedy, putting the blame on Cuba; and the other unleashed at the same time, to cover up all traces of the assassination plan.

Claudia Furiati: Finally, was Oswald in Mexico or not?

Fabián Escalante: I am certain that he went. Anyway, whether it was him or a double, the objective was the same: to travel to Cuba. Could someone other than Oswald apply for a transit visa to Cuba and a visa to return to the Soviet Union? Could anyone imagine that Oswald was not clearly identifiable to the KGB? If his objective was to visit Cuba — because that was an essential part of the plan — how was it possible to send a double to Cuba?

I imagine from what we have seen that if Oswald could have traveled to Cuba and if this trip could have been well documented, that would have been the proof that was needed to implicate Cuba. But let's return to the facts that are known: the Warren Commission Report confirms that various persons said they conversed with Oswald on his way to Mexico. It would have been relatively simple to verify these accounts with a photograph, but they didn't. Afterwards came the story of the Soviet and Cuban Embassies, where Oswald left six photographs. A young Mexican secretary in the Cuban Embassy was the one who received the visa application, duly signed and with six photos. When Oswald realized that he could not obtain the Cuban visa without the Soviet visa, he demanded to see the Cuban consul Eusebio Azcue, whom he then tried unsuccessfully to convince. Due to his aggressive attitude, Oswald was expelled from the building.

Later the investigators from the House of Representatives learned of and accepted Azcue's version that the person who was in the consulate was not Oswald, but they did not consider four fundamental elements: the version of the secretary, Silvia Durán; the photographs submitted, which are of Oswald; his signature, which appears on the application and which is easy to verify; and that he was interviewed by a Soviet consul who was a KGB official, and who could have identified with relative ease the Oswald who lived in the Soviet Union for two years. Remember once again that the person responsible for anti-Cuba operations in Mexico was David Phillips.

Claudia Furiati: Was there any Cuban agent in the CIA's base of operations in Miami in 1963 who knew of the plan to assassinate Kennedy?

Fabián Escalante: We had several agents. Not only there, but also in other places. None of them knew of the plan, because if we had found out we would have alerted the U.S. authorities as it was a question of principles. But I can cite two very illustrative anecdotes: that of Juan Felaifel, who was [a Cuban agent] operating in 1963 in the midst of the Special Missions Group of the CIA in Miami. His brother Anis Felaifel, was a person of confidence and the head of intelligence for Manuel Artime. To quote part of Juan's confidential report to us: "When the assassination of Kennedy occurred in Dallas, Texas, and given the earlier propaganda against him, great joy was expressed by the exiled Cubans and the CIA officials. They declared that now they would take firm steps against the Cuban revolution, something that the heads of the CIA task force in Miami themselves made public. This joy was demonstrated in the behavior of "Robert," a high official of this task force, of Italian descent, who at the moment the assassination took place in Dallas, was with us in a safe house in Miami, watching the President's motorcade on television. At that time, when the announcer reported the death of Kennedy, he exclaimed, 'We finally got the pinko out of the White House!' " Something similar occurred with the individual "Harold Benson" when in 1968, he told our agent "Noel" that, because of Kennedy, Cuba had not been freed of communism and for that reason he felt a fierce hatred for John F. Kennedy. He claimed that after the President's death, he went to Arlington Cemetery to urinate on his grave.

Claudia Furiati: Could it be argued that Cuba, by presenting these versions of the Kennedy assassination, is trying to create a provocation within the United States at an inappropriate moment?
Fabián Escalante: Because there's a new president in the United States? Well, it can be demonstrated perfectly how all this evolved. The CIA must know also, everyone knows. You arrived in Cuba at the beginning of 1992 with the intention of writing a book on the Kennedy case when nobody had the slightest idea that Clinton would be the Democratic Party candidate, much less that he would win the election.

Claudia Furiati: And could there be an implacable counter thesis to this implacable logic?
Fabián Escalante: There is a law of physics: for every action there is a reaction; and obviously, a reaction means a contradiction. But if somebody in the United States wants to, I think it would be very interesting and productive to establish a debate on this topic. I don't declare that I, in particular, am in possession of any great truth. What we did was investigate, think, analyze and tie up loose ends. We didn't start from abstract theories, but rather from the U.S. investigations themselves. You can see from these investigations and commissions that whenever someone gets close to the door to the truth, it is closed. They develop dozens of counter-propaganda operations to avoid being discovered. That was what happened, for example, to Mark Lane, Jim Garrison, Gaetón Fonzi and other investigators.

This book you have written contains a thesis with considerable evidence which can be substantiated. If anyone wants to debate us and make a serious contribution, we are willing to continue the debate. If they want to show something that contradicts what we have said, let them prove it. If anybody wants to defend it, let them defend it. But there is no doubt that they can and will invent anything.

POSTSCRIPT

Case closed?

So our case has come to an end, but we have found only a web of intrigue. I know that endless stories upset those who like definitive endings. The fact that this case is still open is the fault of those who wanted to smother it with confusion in the Warren Commission. Remember that three years later, in 1967, District Attorney Jim Garrison bravely decided to tell a few things in New Orleans, but people didn't like it and pretended not to hear. In the 1970s, there was further speculation about Kennedy's death in the press and many stories came to the surface. How many stories and how much data — even including the Warren Commission investigations — did the House and Senate committees suppress, classify or hide from the final reports? For the sharp-eyed observer there was very little missing. It was only a matter of focus, grabbing a clue and eliminating any idea that the Kennedy affair was solved. But the "hands-off" people arrived and mysterious papers vanished. Case closed?[79]

When I started out on this path two years ago, I told myself I would follow the tracks and see where they led. Besides, one day

---

[79] A recent book by Gerald Posner, *Case closed,* revives the version of Lee Harvey Oswald as the lone gunman.

next century those crates containing all those documents placed in high shelves or in the basements of the U.S. Congress would be released and perhaps give us the answers we seek. Sometimes I wonder if what I have been seeking is not just a magician's box of illusions. I can recognize how so many ruses have been used to muddle our minds and hinder the investigations of honest researchers. For example, on one occasion, the personnel working for the House Committee on Assassinations was suddenly cut, just at the moment when some of the investigators were uncovering some names and decisive connections about the Kennedy assassination. Committee personnel were dismissed on the random basis of particular star signs!

On completing this book in August 1993, we began on the documentary. But further revelations would emerge from the continuing investigations by General Fabián Escalante. Among those new revelations were the names of the two Cuban gunmen involved in the assassination in Dallas.

What other evidence lies in those boxes gathering dust in the Congress archives? Not being patient, why should I have to wait until 2029 to know the truth, when my youthful zest will probably not be the same.

The fabrication of a "patsy"

With regard to the time Lee Harvey Oswald spent in the Soviet Union, some aspects remain to be clarified. In 1957 he was recruited by U.S. Navy Intelligence with the plan to send him on a mission to the Soviet Union. For that reason, he was assigned as a radar operator to the Atsugi Military Base in Japan, where one of the most sensitive projects of U.S. intelligence was being prepared: the flight of the U-2 "invisible" spy aircraft over Soviet territory. Later, Oswald was assigned to the El Toro Base in California, where he learned Russian. In early September 1959, Oswald left the Navy; but on September 11, while still in El Toro, he received an ID as a special employee of the U.S. Defense Department — a "DD Form 1173." In October, he left New

Orleans, took a boat and ended up in England. After a stop-over in Helsinki he went on to Moscow.

Oswald arrived in the Soviet Union still holding his "DD Form 1173." In the notes about his military life that were released to the public, it is argued that such a form was not applicable to reservists. This could hardly have been an administrative mistake; the only conclusion possible is that Lee Harvey Oswald, at that time, was a "civilian who, while rendering special services abroad, need a military identification."[80] In Moscow, Oswald requested political asylum. The Soviets denied it at first, since there was no plausible reason. Oswald then went to the U.S. Consulate in Moscow, tore up his passport and declared himself a convinced communist. He returned to the hotel where he was staying and tried to commit suicide. For this dramatic performance and with information apparently given to Soviet intelligence, Oswald was granted a temporary residence permit.

Back in the United States in June 1962, with a ticket paid for by the State Department, Oswald settled in Dallas. He got a job at a major armaments factory and was engaged by the FBI as agent number 179, with a $200 monthly wage. By the end of April 1963, Oswald moved to New Orleans and started to work in the Guy Banister cell.

Events of spring 1963
A succession of significant events took place in the spring of 1963, as mentioned by the Cuban State Security Department and other sources:[81]

•In the Pontchartrain camp, near New Orleans, 200 terrorist commandos were being trained by Orlando Bosch, Higino "Nino" Díaz, Pedro Luis Díaz Lanz, Tony Cuesta and Frank Sturgis. Their main mission was to attack the Guantánamo Naval Base, on the east coast of Cuba. On April 25, air missions guided by Sturgis, Bosch and Díaz Lanz took off from Pontchartrain to bomb Cuban refineries. In the middle of 1963, operations were

---

[80] *The Houston Post*, November 22, 1992.
[81] Hinckle, Warren and Turner, William, op. cit. Also Garrison, Jim, op. cit.

targeted against Russian ships heading toward Cuba with the direct participation of Mafia men such as John Martino, assistant to the capo John Roselli.

•On April 29, the Cuban Revolutionary Council (CRC), which grouped counterrevolutionary groups in exile, represented by José Miró Cardona and Tony Varona, broke with the Kennedy administration. They accused the President of treason, because he intended to limit subversive activities against Cuba, which were rapidly escalating. This fact merited a remark in the conclusions of the investigation of the Congress Committee in 1978, where it was stated that Cubans in exile felt betrayed in April 1963 because the U.S. government announced that new plans for the invasion of Cuba would not be approved. In a document published by the anti-Castro Cuban exiles at the end of April, Miró Cardona argued: "The U.S. government policy changed sharply, violently and unexpectedly, in a dangerous way, as it had on that sad occasion of the Bay of Pigs, with no reasonable explanation. . . . This note is a protest against the breach of agreements. . . . In face of this situation, which destroyed the patient two-year work in which I enjoyed the trust of the Council, I find no alternative other than resigning. . ." Orlando Bosch also condemned Kennedy by publishing a pamphlet called "The tragedy of Cuba." As a consequence of the new strategy of the U.S. government, the exile movement was falling apart.

•At a meeting in the tourist resort of Bimini (the Bahamas) during the spring, a select group of CIA, Mafia and anti-Castro figures, in addition to planning yet another attempt to murder Fidel Castro, expressed the desire to kill Kennedy. John Roselli and Carlos Prío were some of the participants in these meetings held on board yachts.

•Also in April 1963, Desmond FitzGerald (head of Special Operations at the CIA) planned to take advantage of the visit that James Donovan and John Nolan (two assistants to Robert Kennedy) would make to Fidel Castro. He impregnated with tuberculosis bacilli the swimsuit that would be given as a gift to the Cuban president. Nolan and Donovan, who were in charge of the negotiations with Fidel Castro for the release of the prisoners of the "brigade 2506" arrested at the Bay of Pigs, were unaware of this scheme.

April was the month in which McGeorge Bundy (Kennedy's National Security Adviser) had established new guidelines to solve the Cuban problem.[82]

•In May, a meeting of the front organization called "Friends of Democratic Cuba" was held in the office of Guy Banister in New Orleans. Among its "chiefs of staff" were extremists such as Carlos Prío, Orlando Bosch, Guillermo and Ignacio Novo Sampol, Jorge Mas Canosa, Eladio del Valle Gutiérrez and Herminio Díaz García. This organization was dismantled 10 days after the Kennedy assassination.

While the conspiracy to eliminate Kennedy was already under way, attempts were made to fabricate a conflict between his government and that of Castro. As President Kennedy began to take control of the activities of anti-Castro groups in Florida, the CIA's undercover operations department further separated itself from governmental control and tried to create an armed confrontation between the United States and Cuba. Concurrently, the anti-Castro Cubans and the Mafia refused to accept the Kennedy solution (the blockade) and tried to press him to put a rapid and drastic end to the Cuban revolution. The Pontchartrain camp played a critical role in the provocations against Cuba and the plans for the invasion of Cuba. The 1978 Committee report described Pontchartrain as the "serpent's egg":

---

[82] From this moment on, McGeorge Bundy would play a prominent role in the search for a dialogue with Cuba. Recently, Carlos Lechuga (Cuba's Ambassador to the United Nations in 1963) has revealed new details about this dialogue. On McGeorge Bundy's request, U.S. Ambassador William Attwood met with Lechuga and asked him to prepare an agenda for discussing bilateral relations. The Cuban government had agreed and Lechuga had the impression that the Kennedys wanted someone in the top echelons of the Cuban government to travel to the United States to continue these negotiations. Lechuga noted that Attwood had received a memorandum from McGeorge Bundy which said that as soon as Kennedy returned from his trip to Dallas he would want a full briefing on the talks with the Cuban Ambassador.

it is there that all the main characters of the Kennedy assassination operation met or connected, including Lee Harvey Oswald and Jack Ruby. But despite the recommendations that the FBI pursue the investigation of Pontchartrain, the Bureau dropped it. The matter was simply filed away.

The conspiracy unfolds

According to the Cuban Department of State Security, the Kennedy assassination was actually planned in the office of Guy Banister. It was necessary to choose a man who would be accused of pulling the trigger and who would state that the assassination was ordered by the Cuban government: Lee Harvey Oswald. The operation comprised six stages in three countries — the United States, Mexico and Cuba.

The first stage began in New Orleans, where Oswald started to create his pro-Castro facade.

The second stage was in Dallas. In September 1963, CIA official David Atlee Phillips made an appointment with Lee Harvey Oswald and Antonio Veciana. The purpose of this meeting was to provide details on Oswald's forthcoming trip to Mexico City so as to coordinate the recruitment of Guillermo Ruiz (Veciana's relative who was working at the Cuban Embassy in Mexico as a commercial attache). The plan was to convince Ruiz to testify that Oswald was a Cuban intelligence agent. The Silvia Odio episode in the last days of September had a complementary purpose: to establish a witness (Silvia Odio) that Oswald was in the company of Cubans who asked for help in overthrowing the Castro government.

The visit to the Odio sisters is a key point in the conspiracy: on the one side, it aimed at presenting Oswald's Cuban counter-face; but is also the stage in which he appears as a unique piece in the checkerboard whose role was to accelerate the confrontation between a faction of Cuban exiles and President Kennedy. The Cuban State Security Department has recently concluded that the two men who were with Lee Harvey Oswald on that occasion were the brothers Guillermo and Ignacio Novo Sampol. It should be noted that the descriptions made by Silvia and Annie Odio to investigator Gaetón Fonzi of the two men that visited them coincides with the characteristics of the Novo Sampol brothers. They said that one of them was short and fat, with brilliant black hair combed to the back and looking like a Mexican, and the other was taller and more outspoken.

Lee Harvey Oswald's trip to Mexico City opens the third stage. From a CIA observation post in front of the Cuban Embassy, organized by David Phillips, the Cuban exile Alberto Rodríguez Gallego photographed every person entering and leaving the Embassy. But somehow, the CIA photos submitted to the Warren Commission were of a man that bore no resemblance to the real Oswald. David Phillips in his book *The night watch* justified this error saying that the CIA could not watch the Cuban and Soviet embassies 24-hours a day, seven days a week; he said the confusion was caused by a subordinate who sent a telex reporting on Oswald's visit, and then denying it. Phillips further stated that the CIA had taped conversations between Oswald and the Soviet Embassy, but that the tape was later destroyed, according to the rules. J. Edgar Hoover, the FBI's director, prepared a report on November 23, 1963, mentioning that the Bureau agents who interrogated Oswald in Dallas had seen photos of Lee Harvey Oswald and listened to the recordings provided by the CIA.

Oswald was seen at the Cuban Embassy by the Consul Euzebui Azcue and the Mexican secretary Silvia Durán as well as by vice-consul Miravel and by Guillermo Ruiz, who acted as an interpreter in the conversation Oswald had with Azcue demanding a Cuban visa. In the form he submitted, Oswald stated that he wanted to spend two weeks or more in Havana. Why should he want to stay so long in another country when his objective was to go to another? And if Oswald went three times to the Cuban Embassy at different times, why was he never photographed?

But the objective was not the trip to Moscow, but for documenting Oswald's stay in Havana, which would confirm that Oswald was briefed for the Kennedy assassination in Cuba.

How can the CIA's extraordinary efforts to muddle the Mexican episode be explained? The scheme to link Oswald to the Cuban government for the Kennedy assassination failed, therefore it was not convenient to present any information about his stay in Mexico. Note that Oswald's photos and visa application form were handed by Cuba to the Warren Commission and later to the Congress Committee. Furthermore, immediately after the assassination, Cuban Embassy secretary Silvia Durán was arrested by order of the CIA and heavily pressured to testify that Oswald maintained relations with Cuban intelligence.

The fourth stage also unfolded in Mexico City a few days after the assassination, highlighting the attempts to recruit Cuban official Guillermo Ruiz. Walking in the direction of the Cuban Embassy, Ruiz's wife was confronted by two Mexicans who threw a roll of money to her feet. She ran away scared. A few yards ahead, other strangers approached her and asked about the money. At that moment, she saw two friends leaving the Embassy and ran towards them calling for help. They went to where Mrs Ruiz had first been approached, but the money and the men had disappeared. Cuban State Security interprets this an attempt aimed at recruiting or blackmailing Ruiz and his wife, by having either witnesses or photos of the money being given to Mrs Ruiz, so that the Cuban official would testify that Oswald was a Cuban agent.

Fifth stage. Unable to use Oswald's attempted trip to the Cuban capital, the CIA decided to fabricate letters sent to him from Havana with instructions for the assassination of President Kennedy. The purpose was to have them as evidence in Oswald's hands after the murder. However, only two of the three letters reached the United States. They were dated November 10, 1963, and were mailed in Havana on November 23. In Dallas, the U.S. Secret Service intercepted one of these letters sent to Oswald signed by "Maria de Rosario Molina." This stated that Oswald had killed President Kennedy under instructions from "Pedro Charles"; that they had met in Miami a few months before and that Oswald had received $7,000 from "Charles" as an advance.

Laboratory tests determined that both letters had been written with the same typewriter.[83]

The third letter, signed by "Jorge", dated November 14 and addressed to "Lee Oswald, Royalton Hotel of Miami," never left Havana. In those days, a letter bomb had exploded in the main Cuban mail exchange and the processing of mail was delayed. When the situation was normalized, on November 26, an employee noticed a letter addressed to Lee Oswald who, at this time, was already known worldwide as Kennedy's alleged murderer.

"Jorge's" letter read: "Dear Lee, . . . the subject you told me about last time in Mexico would be a perfect plan and would weaken Kennedy's bravado. . . . You should take care. . . . When you go to Houston, give my regards to your family. . . . As to the other matter, I hope everything runs perfectly." There are other letters dated after the assassination, dated November 26 and 27, where two supposed Cuban dissidents denounce Oswald as an assassin instructed by Cuban State Security.

The sixth stage is the disinformation campaign waged about the Kennedy case immediately after the assassination. Key to this campaign was the press bureau in Miami run by Frank Sturgis which employed journalists Hal Hendrix, a CIA agent specializing in Latin American affairs, and the brothers Jerry and James Buchanan, who belonged to the International Anti-Communist Brigades. This bureau released reams of "information" linking Oswald to the intelligence services of Fidel Castro in Cuba, Mexico and New Orleans, based mainly on the letters mentioned above. On November 22, the day of Kennedy's assassination, Hal Hendrix sent information on Lee Harvey Oswald to a correspondent in Dallas, presenting him as a Soviet and pro-Castro agent. In an article written by James Buchanan for the *Sun Sentinel* in Pompano Beach, Frank Sturgis declared that Oswald had maintained contacts in Miami with Castro's intelligence services.

---

[83] Warren Commission Exhibit 2763.

As in most pantomines, Oswald never knew his final fate in the script. He was not the main character, just the supporting actor.

Gangsters at Dealey Plaza

Reviewing both their own and the U.S. investigations, the Cuban State Security Department concluded that in addition to Richard Helms, David Phillips and Santos Trafficante, the following people also participated in the plotting of the Kennedy assassination: Sam Giancana, Chicago's powerful mobster; the mafioso head John Roselli; General Charles Cabell; Frank Sturgis; Robert Mahue; Gerry Hemmings; and CIA officer Howard Hunt. In the undercover operations department of the CIA, Hunt and Phillips were the main subordinates to Richard Helms.

Someone who deserves a special mention is Howard Hunt, internationally known as the chief instigator of Watergate. His links to Richard Nixon and Frank Sturgis, partners in the scandal, date back to the 1950s. In 1954, Hunt participated with David Phillips in the overthrow of the Guatemalan government. Years later he would be in charge of organizing the CIA's bases in Miami, leading to his relations with Manuel Artime, Tony Varona, Carlos Prío and Santos Trafficante. There he recruited Cuban exiles for the brigades run by Frank Sturgis. From this time, his path is constantly intertwined with that of the Cuban project.

Howard Hunt was one of the financial supporters of the Pontchartrain camp activities. At that time he lived in Dallas, initiating contacts with Texan oil tycoons. In an interview with investigator Gaetón Fonzi, Frank Sturgis stated that it was Howard Hunt who paid $10,000 for the repair of the plane that Sturgis used in his air missions against Cuba. In the recording of a phone call presented in 1986 during a trial of the Orlando Bosch group, Bosch is heard saying that Howard Hunt was getting support and funds for Pontchartrain.

As Manuel Artime's instructor, Howard Hunt shared responsibility for the AM-LASH operation. Moreover, on November 22, 1963, at the time of Kennedy's assassination, he was with Richard Helms and other CIA officials in a house northwest of Washington, discussing plans for the invasion of Cuba. They even mentioned Manuel Artime and his commandos, who were already prepared in Central America, and another group that would depart from the Dominican Republic.

As for the Mafia's connection to the assassination, we have already mentioned that the 1978 Congress Committee established the probable involvement of "individual members of the Mob" such as Santos Trafficante. But the actual evidence of their participation was not included in the Committee's report. The report emphasized that "it would be indispensable" to have access to "Lee Harvey Oswald or Jack Ruby or both," suggesting a connection and therefore the existence of a conspiracy. The relations between Trafficante and Ruby have been proven by the investigations and documents of Cuban State Security. Thus, in exposing the crime, the "Mafia corridor" clue (Dallas-New Orleans-Miami, uniting capos Jack Ruby and Santos Trafficante) becomes as important as the "Guy Banister office" and the "Pontchartrain camp" clues.

According to the Cuban State Security Department, there were two teams at Dealey Plaza in Dallas. By prior arrangement, they performed separate and different tasks. As mentioned in Chapter 5, one of the teams was under Jack Ruby's command. The other was headed by Frank Sturgis.[84] Ruby coordinated the sniper operation: the Chicago Mafia team comprising David Yaras, Lenny Patrick and Richard Cain; and the anti-Castro Cuban gunmen Herminio Díaz García and Eladio del Valle Gutierrez, both linked to the CIA and the Mob. There were four

---

[84] The book *Double Cross* by Chuck Giancana, Sam Giancana's brother and friend of Santos Trafficante, states that the Dallas operation was carried out by two groups, under the command of Jack Ruby and Frank Sturgis. Giancana was murdered only a few days before testifying before the Church Commission in 1975.

to five shots coming from various positions. Frank Sturgis was in charge of communications — receiving and transmitting information on the movement at Dealey Plaza and the motorcade to the shooters and others. Sturgis was also responsible for killing Oswald after the assassination. Members of his team included Orlando Bosch, Pedro Luis Díaz Lanz and the brothers Guillermo and Ignacio Novo Sampol.

Jack Ruby and his team

The day after the assassination of Kennedy, Carroll Jarnagin, a lawyer who attended the Carousel Club (Jack Ruby's nightclub in Dallas), wrote a letter to FBI director J. Edgar Hoover, reporting a conversation he had heard between Ruby and Oswald, whom he had recognized from the news programs.[85] According to the lawyer, Ruby complained about the problems that the Mob was facing in Dallas and Chicago because of Kennedy. In fact, Texas Governor Connally was blocking all their paths for business. At the same time, Sam Giancana was being followed and monitored by Robert Kennedy's express order. In the summer of 1963, FBI agents followed him everywhere. Another target of the Kennedys' campaign was capo Santos Trafficante.

In 1947, in Chicago, Jack Ruby was always seen in the company of the later powerful boss Sam Giancana and two expert gunmen, the bulky Lenny Patrick and David Yaras. Yaras would become a great friend of Ruby's and he was also one of the gangsters who patronized Havana in the 1950s. In a report of the Senate Committee on organized crime, there is a reference to Yaras as someone who performed undercover functions for the Mafia in Havana. Moreover, when the Warren Commission investigators and the 1978 Congress Committee traced Jack Ruby's telephone calls on the days before Kennedy's assassination, they discovered that he had called Lenny Patrick and Robert "Barney" Baker, both mobsters from Chicago. On November 21, 1963, on the eve of the assassination, "Barney" Baker contacted David Yaras in Miami, in a three-minute phone

---

[85] Warren Commission exhibit 2821.

call.[86] There was some suggestion that this call was made at night, which would make it improbable for Yaras to reach Dallas in time for the assassination; but not impossible.

As for Richard Cain, he was a police detective before 1960, and was Sam Giancana's man in the Chicago police force. In 1960, with the CIA's consent, Cain recruited thugs who spoke Spanish to send to Miami and regions of Central America, where they received training in commando tactics. The CIA spent over $100,000 on this activity. Sam Giancana provided Cain with $90,000 for expenses. Cain was dismissed from the police in that same year, when he was caught wiretapping a telephone. He was also involved with the CIA's and the Mafia's anti-Cuba plans from 1960 on. He was one of the gangsters that capo Santos Trafficante placed at the disposal of Operation 40;[87] and he had also been in Cuba in October 1960, when the poisoned capsules plan was started. Richard Cain also played an important role as a CIA agent in Operation Mongoose.[88]

The other two shooters, Eladio del Valle Gutiérrez (alias "Yito") and Herminio Díaz García, already mentioned in the interview with General Fabián Escalante, were supplied by Santos Trafficante. A citation from *Double Cross* by Chuck Giancana is illuminating: "The other assassins were Cubans, friends of Santos Trafficante. They said that one of them was a former [secret] policeman in Havana, who later became a gangster."

Frank Sturgis and his group

The conclusions of the Cuban State Security Department on the involvement of this group — Sturgis, Díaz Lanz and the Novo Sampol brothers — note the testimony of Marita Lorenz to the Congress Committee. It was Lorenz who said that Lee Harvey Oswald and Díaz met at the house of Orlando Bosch in Miami in

---

[86] U.S. Congress Committee on Assassinations, 1978, page 188. Warren Commission, testimonies, vol. 25, pages 294-5.
[87] See Kohn, Howard, "The Hughes-Nixon-Lansky Connection," *Rolling Stone*, May 20, 1976.
[88] Interview with General Fabián Escalante, December 12, 1993.

September 1963, where they discussed a trip to Dallas. This was before Oswald's visit to the Odio sisters in Dallas, together with Guillermo and Ignacio Novo Sampol. These same individuals, according to Lorenz, also traveled to Dallas in mid-November 1963 and were visited by Jack Ruby in a motel. The investigators of the Commission uncovered more evidence about the participation of Frank Sturgis in Kennedy's assassination, but it was not included in the final report. However, Sturgis himself publicly confessed: "We did Watergate because Nixon wanted to stop the leakage of information on our role in the assassination of Kennedy."[89]

Finally, we can put together three incidents that took place in 1976 that indicate the long-standing ties between the figures of the Sturgis group, coming from Miami and the Pontchartrain camp. In the summer of that year, in the town of Bonao in the Dominican Republic, several commando leaders met to form the CURO (United Command of Revolutionary Organizations), whose objective was to mount new assassination plots and terrorist actions. The principal leader was Orlando Bosch, who established connections with international right-wing terrorist organizations. CURO chiefs had links with the CIA and DINA, the brutal Chilean secret police. Among them were the Novo Sampol brothers.

On September 21, 1976, Chilean Orlando Letelier, former Chilean ambassador to the United States during the Allende government, was killed by a terrorist bomb blast, along with his friend Ronni Moffit. Some investigators discovered that a U.S. citizen living in Chile, Michael Townley, a DINA agent, had arrived in Miami and contacted Cuban exiles associated to CURO.[90] Five men, including Ignacio and Guillermo Novo Sampol, were apparently selected by Townley.

On October 6, 1976, a Cuban civil plane with 73 passengers exploded in the air just after a stop-over in Barbados on the way to Cuba. In messages sent to Miami journalists, CURO claimed

---

[89] *San Francisco Chronicle,* April 7, 1990.
[90] *Washington Post,* May 6, 1978.

responsibility for the attack. Two employees of Luis Posada Carriles (Orlando Bosch's faithful partner) in Barbados confessed that their boss and Bosch had supplied the bombs that were placed on the plane. Later, Venezuelan police found equipment, plans and a map of Washington in Carriles's house, indicating a link between the sabotage of the Cuban plane and the assassination of Letelier. Some time later, when Guillermo Novo Sampol was arrested in Miami for cocaine possession, his diary contained notes related to Pedro Luis Díaz Lanz.

So, this story never ends and spreads its tentacles everywhere.

Epilogue

It was just after 5 p.m. on the afternoon of November 22, 1963. Over the loudspeaker, the voice of the Mother Superior drowned out those of the teachers in the classrooms, silencing the noises of the impatient snapping shut of pencil boxes and brief cases, as the students waited for the final bell. It called for silence, a different silence. Just a moment, "one minute for the death of President Kennedy." Docile or rebellious, the girls complied with the bodiless call, standing for this short but infinite time, without knowing why.

Through my prism I can see each classroom, one by one, intersecting, in so many hallways; the labyrinth persists. I focus on the silence of death, the prisoner of both enchantment and terror. I want to understand it and I cannot accept it. Years have gone by. At a crossroads, I urgently desire to find a way out and break through the silence. To solve the crime. To settle the accounts.

The arrows indicated a relationship between the death of Kennedy and the Cuban project. But it was necessary to retrace the route. As the weeks passed, I perceived the essence of the conspiracy: dangerous schemes with hidden faces, secret contacts that left no footprints. I confronted the strategy of deception, and a series of signposts laid out and loose ends ready to mislead. It was the territory of "intelligence services," the invisible system, a dark zone where everything is a lie and everything is the truth.

Yesterday, today, and in an instant I was embraced by the labyrinth. It was the Kennedy case and it was life itself. The whole universe was in that minute.

Appendix 1

Cuban immigration documents showing the two visits made by
Jack Ruby to Cuba in 1959 when he visited Mafia boss Santos
Trafficante, later a key figure in the CIA's war against Cuba and
in the assassination of President Kennedy

Appendix 2

MINISTERIO DEL INTERIOR
DPTO. SEGURIDAD DEL ESTADO

SECRETO

La Habana, junio 21 de 1962
Año de la Planificación

Jefe de la Sección Q

PLANES DEL IMPERIALISMO CONTRA LA REVOLUCION CUBANA.

Planes de la Agencia Central de Inteligencia Yanki a ejecu
tar por la organización denominada Movimiento de Recuperación Revolucionaria, paralizados con la detención de los
dirigentes de la misma.—

a.— Principal plan.—

███

.— El plan a seguir consistía en lo siguiente:

1.— Lograr la unidad de las estimadas 5 organizaciones
de carácter nacional, es decir: MOVIMIENTO REVOLU-
CIONARIO DEL PUEBLO, MOVIMIENTO DEMOCRATA CRISTIA-
NO, DIRECTORIO REVOLUCIONARIO ESTUDIANTIL, MOVI-
MIENTO REVOLUCIONARIO 30 DE NOVIEMBRE "FRANK PAIS"
y el MOVIMIENTO DE RECUPERACION REVOLUCIONARIA. La
unidad se refería al aspecto militar. El aspecto
civil no se había tenido en cuenta todavía.

La unidad se haría a nivel provincial, nombrando
uno de los 5 coordinadores Jefe Militar de la Pro-
vincia, que luego serían sacados a recibir entrenamien
to antes de empezar a funcionar, conjuntamente con
un hombre de confianza de c/u que sería entrenado
en radiotelegrafía. Mientras durara el entrenamien
to (3 meses) de Estados Unidos vendrían telegrafis
tas provisionales.

████████████████████████████████ sostu
vo entrevistas con los Coordinadores Nacionales
del DRE y el MRP. Este último estaba en conversa-
ciones con los Coordinadores Nacionales del MDC y
del MR-30-11. En el pacto de unidad se incluyó en
principio a RESCATE REVOLUCIONARIO DEMOCRATICO y a
UNIDAD REVOLUCIONARIA, a lo cual se opuso ██████
█████████ por entender que estas dos últimas
son "organizaciones de bolsillo".

La CIA le dió instrucciones a ████████████████
█████████ de entrevistarse con los Coordinadores
Nacionales del MDC y del MR-30-11 personalmente. Si

1962 report of Cuba's State Security Department on CIA-backed
counterrevolutionary groups

Appendix 3

REPUBLICA DE CUBA

MINISTERIO DEL INTERIOR
DPTO. SEGURIDAD DEL ESTADO

```
E. M. G. - F. A. R.
      (Jefatura)
E N T R A D A
No. /5 7 Hora:/405
Fecha:    1 3 ENE. 1963
```

La Habana, 17 de enero de 1963
"AÑO DE LA ORGANIZACION"

Del : Ministro del Interior
A   : Dirección Nacional

Ast : Sobre la estrategia y táctica imperialista. Incremento de
la actividad contrarrevolucionaria interna. Auge del ban-
didismo. Política de infiltración y aislamiento de Cuba.

La actividad de las organizaciones y dirigentes contrarrevolucionarios en el exterior iban a revelar una vez más el estado de des-
composición y desunión reinante en las filas contrarrevoluciona-
rias. La principal de las contradicciones se iba a manifestar dentro de la misma Brigada 2506 ▓▓▓▓▓▓▓▓▓▓▓ que fueron realizadas durante la pasada sema
na sobre la ambición desmedida de los "dirigentes" del exilio a
los que calificaba además de elementos carentes de ideales y ter-
minaba planteando la disolución de la Brigada 2506 por haber cum-
plido sus fines.

Esta declaración fue contestada por la "dirigencia" de la Brigada,
compuesta por Artime y compañía, declarando que la misma era una
organización militar y que como tal estaban en este momento "de
permiso".

Al parecer, ni las declaraciones de Kennedy conminando a los gu-
sanos a lograr la unidad, lograban limar asperezas en las campa-
ñas de la "batalla de Miami". Entre las organizaciones contrarre
volucionarias existían profundas y difíciles contradicciones que
no se podían resolver fácilmente.

No obstante la anterior contradicción surgida en el seno de la
brigada mercenaria, el imperialismo y las agencias yanquis conti
nuaban prestando todo su apoyo publicitario y efectivo a la misma. A fines de semana, aparecía mencionado la visita de los inte
grantes de la Jefatura de los mercenarios a Washington para entrevistarse con el encargado de los asuntos de Cuba, Sterlin J.
Cotrell, quien fue recientemente designado por Kennedy para que
coordinara los planes respecto a Cuba. Se mencionaba las informa
ciones públicas en que el objetivo del viaje de los mercenarios
era el de presentar un plan sobre Cuba.

A través de ▓▓▓▓▓▓▓▓▓▓▓▓▓▓▓▓▓▓ recibida en el transcur
so de la semana, en una fuente ligada a la alta dirigencia de la

1963 report of Cuba's State Security Department on the strategy
being used by the CIA against Cuba

Appendix 4

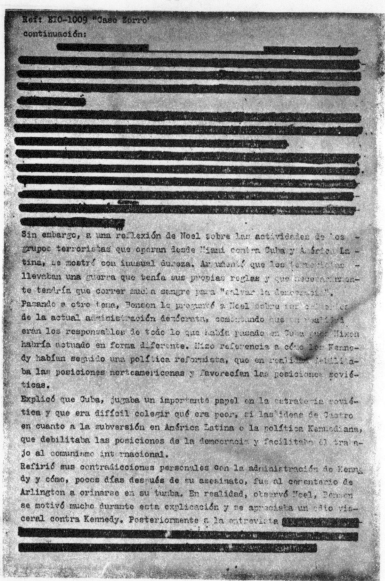

Ref: ETO-1009 "Caso Zorro"
continuación:

[text redacted]

Sin embargo, a una reflexión de Noel sobre las actividades de los
grupos terroristas que operan desde Miami contra Cuba y América Latina, se mostró con inusual dureza. Argumentó que los terroristas
llevaban una guerra que tenía sus propias reglas y que necesariamen-
te tendría que correr mucha sangre para "salvar la democracia".
Pasando a otro tema, Benson le preguntó a Noel sobre sus opiniones
de la actual administración demócrata, comentando que en realidad
eran los responsables de todo lo que había pasado en Cuba y que Nixon
habría actuado en forma diferente. Hizo referencia a cómo los Kennedy habían seguido una política reformista, que en realidad debilitaba las posiciones norteamericanas y favorecían las posiciones sovié-
ticas.
Explicó que Cuba, jugaba un importante papel en la estrategia soviética y que era difícil colegir qué era peor, si las ideas de Castro
en cuanto a la subversión en América Latina o la política Kennediana,
que debilitaba las posiciones de la democracia y facilitaba el trabajo al comunismo internacional.
Refirió sus contradicciones personales con la administración de Kennedy y cómo, pocos días después de su asesinato, fue al cementerio de
Arlington a orinarse en su tumba. En realidad, observó Noel, Benson
se motivó mucho durante esta explicación y se apreciaba un odio visceral contra Kennedy. Posteriormente a la entrevista [redacted]

[text redacted]

Report of Cuba's State Security Department and its agent "Noel"
on the CIA's "Harold Benson"

Appendix 5

CONSULADO DE CUBA, MÉXICO, D.F.

Solicitud de visa No.: _779_

Fecha: 27 de septiembre de 1963.

Nombre: Lee Harvey Oswald

Ciudadanía _norteamericana_

Fecha y lugar de nacimiento: Octubre 18, 1939 en New Orleans, U.S...

Pasaporte No. D-092526

Dirección permanente: _____ 4907 Magazine St. New Orleans, La., U.S.A.

Ocupación (expresando empresa para la que trabaja) Fotógrafo Comercial

Estancias anteriores en Cuba ---

Motivos de las estancias anteriores ---

Familiares o personas conocidas residentes en Cuba __

10 OCT. 1963

Ha sido invitado desde Cuba? (Sí:) (No: x)

Con que objeto? ----

Cual es el motivo del viaje propuesto viaje de tránsito para la Unión Soviética

semanas
lo mismo 2 semanas y si es posible mas tiempo.

Fecha propuesta de llegada a Cuba septiembre 30 de 1963

Dirección en Cuba:

(firma del interesado

PARA USO DE LA MISION

OBSERVACIONES El solicitante dice ser miembro del P.C. Norteamericano y Secretario en New Orleans del Fair Play for Cuba Committee. Y que vivió en la Unión Soviética desde Octubre de 1959 al 19 de junio de 1962; que allá se casó con una ciudadana soviética. Mostró documentación que lo acredita como miembro de las dos organizaciones mencionada y acta de matrimonio. Se presentó en la Embajada de la URSS en esta ciudad pidiendo que su visa sea enviada a dicha Embajada en Cuba. Nosotros llamamos al Consulado de la URSS y nos contestaron que ellos tenían que esperar la autorización de Moscú para darle la visa y que tardaría alrededor de 4 meses.

Lee Harvey Oswald's visa application form submitted to Cuban Embassy in Mexico in September 1963. Oswald was denied a visa to visit Cuba.

Appendix 6

REPUBLICA DE CUBA

MINISTERIO DEL INTERIOR
DPTO. SEGURIDAD DEL ESTADO

La Habana, 23 de Noviembre de 1976
" AÑO DEL XX ANIVERSARIO DEL GRANMA "

Informe especial

En _____ informó lo siguiente :

VECIANA es un agente especial de LA CIA, que trabaja para ha
cer " dirty jobs ". Su jefe es un tal MAURICE BISHOP que ba
jo otro nombre estuvo en Cuba en 1959-60. Ella estima que en
tonces BISHOP se hacía pasar como ciudadano o comerciante -
belga.

_____ VECIANA le expresó en una ocasión, que él -
sabe la CIA asesinó a KENNEDY y que BISHOP esta enredado en
ese asunto. Agrega que éste nunca le quiso dar detalles al -
respecto, pero que ultimamente ha podido comprobarlo, ya que
en 1973 encontrándose _____, donde BISHOP fue a ver a VECIANA,-
oyó que discutían acaloradamente, _____
_____ claramente que VECIANA juraba que nunca-
diría una palabra del asunto, BISHOP sin embargo le propuso-
que aceptara ir a la cárcel y que le daría además $ 300 mil-
dólares. Más tarde VECIANA fue enviado a la prisión, acusado
por el tráfico de drogas _____
pero una vez que se había tomado unas copas le dijo " es mejor que acepte la cabronada y vaya a la cárcel, total 18 meses pasan rápidos y es mejor estar vivo que muerto, además -
esos dólares no vienen mal."

Report of Cuba's State Security Department on CIA agent Tony
Veciana and the CIA's "Maurice Bishop"

Appendix 7

SECRETO

REPUBLICA DE CUBA

MINISTERIO DEL INTERIOR
DPTO. SEGURIDAD DEL ESTADO

"Muy Secreto" ... cont... informe del agente Neno.   pág.10

Al producirse la Crisis de Octubre, en sus primeros momentos, existió
preocupación dentro del exilio por la actitud que asumiría el Presidente
frente al comunismo, hecho que fue reflejado en la prensa y concretamente
en los periódicos Patria y Miami Herald, disipándose esta preocupación
transitoriamente cuando el Presidente declaró la cuarentena a Cuba, momento en que dentro de los apátridas y los mandos de la CIA se pensó que
era el preludio de la invasión, valorándose esta acción de Kennedy como
de apoyo al exilio.

Sin embargo, a las pocas horas, al correrse los rumores de que se había
llegado a un acuerdo por el cual Kennedy no invadiría Cuba, se consideró
en los medios exiliados y de la CIA como una nueva traición del Presidente.

Como consecuencia de los acuerdos que ponen fin a la Crisis de Octubre,
se incrementó el control sobre los grupos contrarrevolucionarios, así -
como otras actividades que controlaba la base operativa de la CIA en --
Miami, creándose por estas medidas un resentimiento mayor entre los oficiales, los dirigentes exiliados y los apátridas en general, que opinaban
que Kennedy simpatizaba con el establecimiento de un Estado Socialista en
Cuba, lo que unido a la intromisión de Robert Kennedy en los asuntos de
la CIA y la Mafia, creó un climax en contra de los hermanos Kennedy.

Al producirse el asesinato de Kennedy, en Dallas, Texas y dada la propaganda anterior contra él mismo, se manifestó una gran alegría entre los
exiliados cubanos y los oficiales de la CIA. Estos manifestaron que --
ahora sí se darían pasos firmes contra la Revolución Cubana, asunto este
que daban a la publicidad los propios jefes del grupo operativo de la
CIA en Miami. Esa alegría se demostró en la actuación del oficial "Robert"
alto dirigente de esa unidad operativa, de descendencia italiana, el --
cual, en los momentos en que se producía el asesinato en Dallas, se en-
contraba junto a nosotros en una casa de seguridad en Miami viendo el -
paso del Presidente por la televisión. En esta ocasión, en un arranque
de júbilo cuando el locutor anunció la muerte de Kennedy, exclamó: "Al
fin eliminamos al rosado de la Casa Blanca".

Pocos días después en la entrevista que sostuve con ▇▇▇▇▇▇▇▇
                            informé del asunto mencionado,

1963 report of Cuba's State Security Department and its agent
Juan Felaifel (agent "Neno") on the activities of the CIA

Appendix 8

MINISTERIO DEL INTERIOR
DPTO. SEGURIDAD DEL ESTADO

pág ... 14
"Secreto"

Esto último parece constituir su verdadero objetivo, ya que su
estancia, aunque fuera por breve tiempo, era imprescindible
para "legalizar" las relaciones que más tarde servirían de ar-
gumentos. En la práctica esa oportunidad podía ser aprovechada
para dejar fuertes señales que mostraran posteriormente sus -
vínculos con Cuba.

En el consulado cubano se le hizo saber al solicitante por la
empleada mexicana Silvia Durán, que, de acuerdo con los proce-
dimientos usuales, su solicitud tenía que ser tramitada con el
MINREX en La Habana y además tendría que obtener la visa de -
entrada en la Unión Soviética. El visitante insistió, expresan
do de forma airada y descompuesta su contrariedad.

Ante esta solicitud intervino el cónsul Eusebio Ascue'para rei-
terarle las explicaciones sobre la demora en los trámites, adop
tando el norteamericano una actitud grosera, lo que obligó a -
Azcue a solicitarle que abandonara el recinto consular.

Estos hechos indican la intención de que quede fijada su visita
a la vez garantiza que sea recordado.

El 7 de octubre fue recibida en el MINREX de Cuba la solicitud
de visa y examinada conforme a normas establecidas y el día 15
de octubre se instruyó al consulado en México que le sería en-
tregada la visa cuando obtuviera el permiso de entrada al país
de destino.

En el anexo 1 aparecen los documentos sobre la visita al consulado y la correspondencia dirigida al Gobierno cubano por la --
Comisión Warren sobre ese tema.

1978 report of Cuba's State Security Department investigation
into the Kennedy assassination

Appendix 9

Documents in possession of Cuba's State Security Department showing that Eladio del Valle — now named as one of those who shot President Kennedy — was an agent of Batista's secret police

Appendix 10

San José, Costa Rica. — SÁBADO 18 DE MAYO DE 1957.

La República

PRECIO DEL EJEMPLAR: ¢ 0.25 — Miembro de la Sociedad Interamericana de Prensa (SIP) — EDICION DE HOY: 24 PAGINAS.

...PTURADOS.

TRES PISTOLEROS TRUJILL

CONTRATADOS PARA ATENTAR CONTRA LA VIDA DEL PRESIDE
DE CIUDAD TRUJILLO VOLARON A MANAGUA Y LUEGO DE PERMANECER CUATRO DIAS ALLI ARRIBAR AEROPUERTO DE "EL COCO".

Jesús González Cartas (a) "El Extraño" había entrado al servicio de Trujillo y obtenido el grado de General recibien
mo" de una pistola calibre 45 con culata de oro en la que se destacan las estrellas del genera
Los servicios de inteligencia del gobierno les siguieron la pista desde el día de su llegada y pudieron observar todos sus
...ra el día de ayer hacían solicitado entrevista con el Pdte. Figueres como "exilados cubanos"

DOS MIL CONDENADOS A LA HORCA EN HUNGRIA
El informe lo recibió el Secretario General de la ONU Dag Hammarskjold. Los niños húngaros son enviados al campo de concentración en Qbunda por el "delito" de usar cintas negras en los brazos el día 23 de cada mes en conmemoración del día que inició la revolución contra la tiranía comunista (TEXTO EN PAGINA 8)

...rjeta de turismo se co...
...nenta favorablemente
las facilidades ofrecidas por los ...mes centroamericanos para el ...no de turistas expuestas en la ...vención de la ASTA en Guata...cala se destacó la Tarjeta de ...rismo de nuestro país, PAG 7)

GAL HACER DEDUCCI...ES AL DECIMO TERCER MES
Intención del legislador al es...lecer el beneficio del décimo...cer que quienes disfruten de ...n sueldo adicional gocen del mo para enfrentarse a los gas extraordinarios de fin de año ...nciamiento del Ministerio de Trabajo (PAGINA 7)

Juan Manuel Delgado (a) El Francés es piloto de la Línea Aérea Dominicana
Ayer a las cinco y media de la tarde las autoridades realizaron la sensacional captura de los tres pistoleros. Centenares de personas se congregaron en torno al Hotel "Oasis" atraídos por el formidable movimiento policial y de radio patrullas que rodearon la manzana, en conocimiento de la gran peligrosidad de los tres sujetos

Declaraciones del Ministro de Seguridad Pública

SENSACIONAL INFORMACION DE 'LA REPUBLICA' — (TEXTO EN PAGINA 24)

HERMINIO DIAZ
... llegó primero...

JESUS GONZALEZ CARTAS
...Jefe de los Confabulados...

JUAN MANUEL DELGADO
.. de la Línea Aérea Dominicana...

Newspaper coverage in Costa Rica in May 1957 showing Herminio Díaz. The Cuban State Security Department has now named Herminio Díaz as one of those who shot President Kennedy on behalf of the Mafia and the CIA

INDEX

MIRR (Insurrectional Movement
for the Recovery of the
Revolution), 69, 77, 133, 147
Missile Crisis, 8, 44, 54-60, 62, 63,
67, 78, 93, 97, 101, 113, 122, 127,
130, 131
Mohrenschildt, George de, 74, 75
MRP (People's Revolutionary
Movement), 35, 36, 38, 50, 82, 88,
123
MRR (Revolutionary Recovery
Movement), 17, 22, 49, 52

—N—

National Security Council (U.S.),
14, 16, 20, 21, 41, 52, 58, 62, 92,
129
Naval Intelligence, 72, 74, 76, 118,
148
Nicaragua, 28, 29, 53, 54, 68, 70,
115, 148
Nixon, Richard, 7, 14, 20, 21, 30,
34, 90, 94, 119, 120, 142, 162,
165, 166
"Noel", 14, 145, 146, 151, 172
Noel, James, 14
Novo Sampol, Guillermo and
Ignacio, 132, 139, 157-59, 164-67

—O—

O'Connell, Jim, 23, 24, 25, 118
Odio, Amador, 38
Odio, Silvia, 38, 81, 82, 88, 89, 122,
124, 125, 158
Opa-locka, 27
Operation 40, 12, 14, 16, 19, 20,
132, 133, 147-48, 165
Operation AM-LASH, 64, 66, 69,
117, 121, 163
Operation Liborio, 34, 37, 53, 82,
95, 131, 145
Operation Mongoose, 4, 39, 41-47,
50- 55, 61, 62, 66, 67, 77, 96-98,

104, 112, 119, 120, 127, 130, 135,
140, 143, 165
Operation Patty (Candela), 34, 36,
95, 145
Operation Peter Pan, 34, 37, 43, 144
Operation Pluto, 4, 20, 21, 23, 28,
94, 103, 112, 119, 143
Operation Zapata, (see also Bay of
Pigs) 22, 28
Operation ZR Rifle (see ZR Rifle)
Organization of American States
(OAS), 37, 42, 77
Orozco Crespo, Miguel Angel, 54
Oswald, Marina, 81, 88

—P—

Paine, Ruth, 81, 88, 109
Panama, 18, 53, 115, 147
Patrick, Lenny, 163-64
Peking restaurant, 27, 48
Pérez Díaz, Bartolomé, 48
Pérez San Román, José, 29
Phillips, David Atlee, 15, 16, 20, 22,
49, 87, 88, 123, 130-36, 139, 142-
147, 149, 150, 158, 159, 162
Pontchartrain camp, 77, 78, 133,
135, 136, 139, 147, 149, 155, 157,
158, 162, 163, 166
Posada Carriles, Luís, 135, 146,
147, 167
Powers, Francis Gary, 73, 126
Prío Socorrás, Carlos, 17, 18, 25, 26,
67, 114, 139, 142, 156-57, 162
Project Cuba, 42, 119
Prouty, Colonel Fletcher, 103, 104

—R—

Ray Rivero, Manuel, 35, 36, 57, 82
"Rescate", 26, 27, 28, 48, 49, 140
Roselli, John, 8, 24-26, 28, 47, 49,
117, 118, 120, 121, 126, 130, 141,
142, 147, 156, 162

Also published by Ocean Press

THE CUBAN REVOLUTION AND THE UNITED STATES
A chronological history
by Jane Franklin
An invaluable resource for scholars, teachers, journalists, legislators, and anyone interested in international relations, this volume offers an unprecedented vision of Cuba-U.S. relations.

AFROCUBA
An anthology of Cuban writing on race, politics and culture
edited by Pedro Pérez Sarduy and Jean Stubbs
What is it like to be Black in Cuba? Does racism still exist in a revolutionary society which claims to have abolished it? How does the legacy of slavery and segregation live on in today's Cuba?

GUANTÁNAMO: THE BAY OF DISCORD
The story of the U.S. military base in Cuba
by Roger Ricardo
This book presents a clear, concise history and the continuing controversy over the control and ownership of Guantánamo.

CRUEL AND UNUSUAL PUNISHMENT
The U.S. blockade of Cuba
by Mary Murray
Is Washington's trade ban with Cuba an embargo, as the U.S. government claims, or an illegal blockade? Does the policy violate international law, the UN Charter and the principles of the Organization of American States? This book will help you make up your mind.

FACE TO FACE WITH FIDEL CASTRO
A conversation with Tomás Borge
One of the most important books to emerge from Latin America in the 1990s, this is a lively dialogue between two of the region's most controversial political figures.

For a list of Ocean Press distributors, see copyright page